Guide For the Presiding Officer

A Functional Guide for Presidents and Chairmen

Second Edition

Joyce L. Stephens

Frederick Publishers
Clearwater, Florida

Copyright © 1991, 1997 by Joyce L. Stephens

Library of Congress Catalog Card Number: 97-061140

ISBN 0-9629765-6-3

GUIDE FOR THE PRESIDING OFFICER
A FUNCTIONAL GUIDE FOR PRESIDENTS AND CHAIRMEN
SECOND EDITION

Biblio.
Reading List
Index.

Frederick Publishers
P. O. Box 5043
Clearwater, FL 33758
813-530-3978

Printed in the United States of America

Foreword
To First Edition

When Jo poses the provocative question, "Now what?"— be prepared!! Be prepared for the answers to questions that passed briefly through your mind when you consented to becoming a nominee. Be prepared for the answers to questions that were definitely in mind when you considered acquiring this manual. And, by all means, be prepared for the answers to questions that prior to this time had never entered your mind at all.

Jo has shared a wealth of knowledge gleaned from her personal experiences in the avenues of studying, teaching, presiding, serving as a professional parliamentarian, lecturing, and writing. It behooves the reader not only to peruse this manual, but to consult it as often as possible in order to receive the full advantages intended by the author.

True to the tradition of a registered parliamentarian, Jo offers advice. If you use this manual to its fullest advantage, you will no doubt come to feel that you have your own personal PRP serving as advisor. You will *learn from* this advice—you will *subscribe to* this advice—you will *grow with* this advice.

Marjorie Humphreys Park
Professional Registered Parliamentarian

Preface

In 1984 when *Basic Parliamentary Procedure Workbook* was published, it was a meager volume. By the time the third edition was published in 1990, the Workbook had expanded into a usable size. The success of the Workbook, now in its fifth edition, is greater than the author ever expected. The book is used by students of parliamentary procedure in numerous states as a learning aid in preparation for taking examinations. Public acceptance is rewarding as well, as the book is used by ever-increasing numbers of organizations and individuals.

During the years since the Workbook was published, many new officers have requested something more comprehensive for their particular use. From the author's experience in chairing meetings and serving as a professional for many diverse groups, *Guide For The Presiding Officer* originated. Only experience can offer the background to make such a book credible. This second edition of the book is a testament to the need and the requests for help with this important task.

The task of chairing meetings is a difficult undertaking. This becomes quite evident when the assembly is diverse in opinion or predisposed to conflict. The chapter on *tips for the new president* will help to make chairing your first meeting much easier. This edition offers some additional tips. This book provides the language of the presiding officer to aid the president in chairing even the most difficult meetings. The Guide is for inexperienced presiding officers as well as for more experienced chairmen who wish to improve their leadership skills. There are helpful hints throughout and the author has placed special bits of information in boxes at the end of other text.

To cover all situations which could occur in meetings is not possible. However, the author has endeavored to cover the most frequently reported, and is grateful to all who have made suggestions for the Workbook and the Guide. They have contributed greatly to the content. Everyone is welcome to comment to the author on any of her books. Perhaps your suggestion will appear the next edition.

Some of the material in the Guide is expanded from the Workbook. However, it is not feasible in these pages to include all the information from the Workbook. The author anticipates that the books will be used side by side for the greatest benefit.

The text is self-explanatory. The information supplied is, however, supplemental to your association documents, and should be used accordingly. The book is written in simple language, using Robert's Rules of Order Newly Revised, 1990 edition, as the primary authority for its parliamentary information.

For Steve and Juliet

Acknowledgments

The author is grateful to the following individuals who helped with this second edition of the book as well as the first edition: Sankey F. Stephens, Jr., critical reader, editor, and accountant; Juliet Stephens Tripp, who contributed greatly to the design of the book; Heidi Tilney Kramer, environmental artist, for her clever drawings; Rema J. Likeness, Linda G. Young and other non-parliamentarians who have recently served as officers in homeowner associations, church boards, PTA, and professional associations; Mary Abel for her valuable suggestions; and Marjorie Humphreys Park, PRP, for her assistance with the first edition. The author also wishes to thank the organizations for which she has chaired meetings professionally. They have given her valuable experience in chairing meetings for unfamiliar groups of people. And thank you to the many individuals who have called or written to her about the book after having seen it in the local library or purchased it from catalogs or book stores. These individuals and groups have added valuable advice for this second edition.

Introduction to the Second Edition

Five months after publication, *Guide For the Presiding Officer* appeared on the best seller list for a major library distributor. The author has been very gratified by the response to the book. These responses have come from many countries, including Canada when a reader who called said that the library would let her check out the book for only three weeks, she needed it longer than that, and she wanted her own copy. This response is typical of the many who have telephoned or written to the author about the book.

Since the first edition was published in 1991, the author has received suggestions from other parliamentarians and requests from presiding officers for additional material. In response to these suggestions and requests, this second edition is expanded to meet these needs.

Material added includes tips and examples, a page on small board procedure, additional paragraphs in existing chapters, scripts for conventions and for chairing a revision of the bylaws, and additional "dibbles."

Dibble: A tool for making holes in which to plant seeds.

The Author

Joyce L. Stephens
Professional Registered Parliamentarian
Parliamentary Specialist
Certified Teacher

Joyce L. Stephens was awarded a Certificate of Registration in 1980 by examination of the National Association of Parliamentarians, and achieved the designation of Professional the same year. She is certified by The Academy of Parliamentary Procedure and Law as Parliamentary Specialist and Certified Teacher. Her certifications are the highest which can be achieved by both organizations. She has served as National President of the Academy and as President of the Florida State Association of Parliamentarians. She is currently State Parliamentarian for the Florida State Association of Parliamentarians, National Parliamentarian for the Academy. She is a member of the Professional Development Committee of The National Association of Parliamentarians, the committee that administers the qualifying and recertification of Professional Registered Parliamentarians, and has served on the NAP Board of Directors. She graduated from Eckerd College (formerly Florida Presbyterian College) with a degree in management. She is a member colleague of CAI (Community Associations Institute). She is author of books on parliamentary procedure and articles in several publications, and is the editor of *The Answer*, the journal of the Academy, and of *The Florida Parliamentarian,* the quarterly magazine of the Florida State Association of Parliamentarians. She is a State of Florida certified Provider of Continuing Education for Community Association Managers, and a consultant for the Florida Institute of Government at the University of South Florida. She has been adjunct faculty at Daytona Community College. She has extensive experience in all phases of parliamentary law and procedure having served as a parliamentary consultant for over seventeen years. She has served in numerous offices in professional, civic, and charitable associations, acquiring the kind of organizational experience which cannot be acquired in any other way. She has performed all parliamentary services to conventions, professional associations, fraternal associations, homeowners associations, churches, credit unions, labor unions, sports organizations, historical societies, and other not for profit organizations.

Other publications in print by the same author available from
Frederick Publishers:
Basic Parliamentary Procedure Workbook, 5th ed.
Guide to Voting: Procedures For Voluntary Organizations
Bylaws: Writing, Adopting, Amending
Guide to Elections: Procedures for Voluntary Organizations
Parliamentary Miscellany
Copyright Basics for Teachers and Newsletter Editors
Leadership Series of Monographs

Contents

Contents

Dibbles

Tips for the New President

"Cheshire Puss," she [Alice] began... "would you please tell me which way I ought to go from here?" "That depends on where you want to get to," said the cat. *Lewis Carroll*

You have accepted the nomination for president. Now what? You know the general duties of the president of your organization—administrative duties that you have observed and shared with other members probably as a board member or as a vice president. Chairing meetings is another matter. Presiding is an honor and will be rewarding. Nevertheless, you will gain more self-confidence and do a better job if you follow a few simple steps to prepare yourself.

Before Chairing a Meeting

✔ Know that when chairing a meeting as president, concentrating on procedure and the content of the business at the same time is difficult. This will become easier with practice, as the procedure becomes more and more automatic.

✔ **Be thoroughly prepared.** Know your bylaws. Every provision of the bylaws is there for a reason and will be important as time goes by. Meetings must be conducted according to this document. Bylaws are a set of limitations on how the organization will go about taking care of business. Do not rely on your parliamentarian or other adviser to know these rules for you. If your organization is incorporated, study the provisions of the articles of incorporation. If your organization is a constituent division of a larger organization, study all the superior body's rules that apply to your local group. Bring with you to meetings: bylaws and other rules, minutes of the previous meeting, and other needed documents such as membership or committee lists. The recording secretary should have available at least a year's minutes in case there is a need for research during the meeting.

✔ If your organization is a **nonprofit corporation**, you will benefit from a reading of the statutes regarding nonprofit corporations in your state. Reading the statutes will give you a basis for answering questions when they arise, and will help you when you discuss matters with the organization's attorney. You will have enough knowledge to advise the organization that a particular question is one to ask the attorney. Unions have applicable federal laws, condominiums have state statutes, and other groups have rules. Ask your association attorney to point out by statute number or name which ones apply to your organization.

✔ **Write an agenda.** This sounds like simple advice. However, when you write down each item of business, leave a few spaces for notes. Write in everything that is expected to happen at the meeting. If you anticipate resistance to a proposed action, write in all the officers, committee chairmen, and others who may be called on to answer questions. If there are motions from the board to come before the membership meeting, write in the wording of the motions on your agenda. That way you will never lose your place on the agenda while looking for small pieces of paper on which you have written notes. Write into your agenda the wording of any simple bylaws amendments. If you distribute your agenda to other officers and the minutes approval committee, they will be able to follow the business more closely and accurately. The Recording Secretary will benefit from your detailed agenda and the process of recording the minutes will be much more simple and accurate. See the sample agenda in Appendix V.

During the meeting check off the items on the agenda as they are completed.

✔ **A script agenda** is a helpful device for the new president. In a script agenda every item of business on the agenda has corresponding language for the presider. Even the most inexperienced chairman can preside with more confidence when the words are there to be used easily without relying upon memory for the wording, and what comes next. A professional can help you write a script agenda that will suit your needs. Practice writing a script agenda using the language provided in this book. The practice will also help you learn the terminology.

✔ **Walk through the meeting**, examining every aspect of the order of business and your agenda. Plan for each item—what you will say to introduce it, what you will do if a motion is made—how you will handle each item. Be prepared for amendments and other motions.

✔ **Know parliamentary procedure.** *There is no substitute for parliamentary procedure in meetings.* The presiding officer should know more about parliamentary procedure than the members. You will not be intimidated by a member who claims knowledge if you are sure of your own knowledge. There are members who will take advantage of a chairman's weakness in this area.

Take a few classes in parliamentary procedure. More than one class is recommended because one will help you to understand the principles of parliamentary procedure, and several will start you on your way to really understanding the purpose of each motion and rule. Every endeavor has its rules. Learning to play golf or tennis or bridge requires numerous hours. Your members deserve no less from you in learning the proper procedure for accomplishing the business of their association.

There are various sources for workshops and classes in procedure. Check your local newspaper for any that are scheduled in your area. Take every opportunity to learn more. Read *Basic Parliamentary Procedure Workbook*. Have our own copy of *Roberts Rules of Order Newly Revised* and refer to it often. Refresh your memory on subjects often.

A professional can set up workshops for your particular group so that other officers and directors will have an opportunity to learn also.

✔ **Before elections and amendment of bylaws,** read that part of the parliamentary authority and your bylaws thoroughly. Some of the most frequent calls received by professional parliamentarians are from organizations in trouble after such major events. Follow the bylaws and parliamentary authority in minute detail. Completed business is less likely to be challenged if great care has been taken in advance.

✔ **When you appoint a parliamentarian** for your meetings, be certain that the individual has a thorough understanding of the rules. That means all the rules, from bylaws to parliamentary law. The parliamentarian's knowledge will be important to you in meetings, and crucial when there is controversy. Don't hesitate to call a professional when needed. Ask your prospective parliamentarian how much he or she has studied procedure and how many classes attended. If you wish to appoint someone who has not had much education in procedure, make sure the appointee takes classes before serving.

✔ **Remind your parliamentarian** that the position requires the same impartiality as that of presiding officer. Neither the parliamentarian nor the president should vote on a matter unless the vote is by ballot. If the chosen individual cannot abide by these guidelines, someone else should be appointed to the position. You will need unbiased opinion when you have questions. The perception of the impartiality of the parliamentarian reflects upon the president.

✔ **Planning** should start on these matters when you first think of becoming a candidate for office. If you have been chosen to serve as a vice president, now is the time to study procedure. Then, when the time comes for you to preside, you will have the knowledge that you need.

✔ **Language of the presiding officer.** Some of the wording in *language for the presiding officer* presented in this book may be unfamiliar to you. Practice until you can say the phrases with comfort and ease. Know where each is used, and don't hesitate to use the proper parliamentary language. You will be pleasantly surprised at how much your reputation will grow when the members hear a well prepared presiding officer chair a meeting correctly. We have all heard some well-known persons in our communities, while presiding, use terminology that is outdated, phrases that do not make sense, and language that relates only to legislative assemblies. Improper language in their presiding has had a tendency to diminish their credibility. Incorrect terminology no doubt became habit as it was passed along from one chairman to another. Don't copy someone else's bad habits! This book will provide you with do's and do not's of such phrases.

✔ **Study the duties** of the president and of all officers, directors, and committees so that you will know who has specific responsibilities and powers. Drawing a structure chart of responsibilities and accountabilities can be very useful.

✔ **Ex officio.** [By virtue of the office] The president is a member ex officio of committees when the bylaws dictate. When the president is a member ex officio, the chairmen must notify the president of meetings just as they do other members of the committees. The president is not required to attend the meetings and is not counted in determining the quorum. The president may make motions and vote in committees when a member ex officio. [In all such phrases, think of what the words mean and you will develop the habit of speaking in correct terminology.]

✔ **When the president appoints.** Appoint persons to committees who have relevant skills. Friendship is not justification to appoint someone to an important post.

✔ **Appoint meeting committees** well in advance of the meeting date, so that they will be thoroughly trained in their duties and will be prepared. When participants know their duties the meeting will run more efficiently and smoothly. For annual meetings and conventions you will require a credentials committee (when voting rights must be established), a standing rules committee, a program committee, a tellers committee, among others. Keep yourself informed of committee work. You don't want any surprises during the meeting. Having a list of all meeting duties with names attached to each duty is helpful.

✔ **Committees for conventions** require training for the jobs they will perform. Make certain that they are trained well in advance of the meetings. For example, the tellers or election committee should have practiced the balloting and counting process so that the votes may be counted quickly without errors which could cause problems later on.

✔ **Protocol.** Your group may be large or small, professional or social. The importance of protocol is for every group regardless of its nature. Most groups at least have guest speakers. Etiquette is a matter of good business as well as good manners. Plan to appoint a protocol chairman who will be prepared to give advice on seating, notices, correspondence, and such other matters of protocol that become necessary. Nothing is more embarrassing to a guest—speaker or dignitary—than a lack of preparation on the part of the organization.

✔ **Keep the vice president informed** about program, agenda, committees, and other plans so that the appropriate person is prepared to chair the meeting if for some reason you will not be able to do so. Emergencies happen, and anticipation of emergencies in the meeting is your responsibility.

✔ **Date everything** that comes across your desk and everything you mail or give to anyone else. Put a name on any paper that you receive that does not bear one. Later you will need to know who sent it to you and when.

✔ **The best presiding officers** possess two traits: complete assurance of their own knowledge, and a self-control that prohibits emotional involvement in the content of the business at hand.

That might seem to suggest that you may not have any interest in the business of your association. That is not possible. You should not *show* your feelings readily while presiding. That too is a matter of practice.

Personal

✔ Your **personal appearance.** Wear tailored clothing, in non-distracting colors, and very little jewelry. Splashy colors are fun, although distracting to the assembly. If you are a woman, avoid fashion fads such as extremely long red fingernails if possible. These adornments detract from your credibility. You want the attention focused on what you are saying, not on what you are wearing. If you are a man, avoid loud patterned jackets and flashy jewelry. These hints might seem trivial to you. In a business meeting, however, especially a controversial one, your credibility is important to your ability to control the meeting.

✔ **Your voice.** A monotone becomes boring fast. A pleasant, well modulated voice will make your meetings more congenial and efficient. Do not become excited and speak in a shrill voice. An excited chairman can throw the meeting into chaos. Remain calm and your voice will be calm. If you are nervous, try breathing in through your nose and out through your mouth with deep breaths several times. A speaker's tip: if your mouth is dry, follow the above advice—if your mouth is wet, reverse the procedure. You cannot be expected to be without emotion. When you feel very emotional, however, ask the vice president to preside.

✔ Do you **look as if you enjoy presiding** and being president? If you do, members will respond more pleasantly to your attitude. Some new presidents think that they must be all business and no fun. The important thing is to be yourself and don't stiffen up after your election.

✔ **Keep your sense of humor.** A sense of humor is a valuable asset.

✔ **Past presidents** can be of help to you in getting started. Nevertheless, you must remember that this is your term of office, and you cannot do things the same way someone else did. Do not allow past presidents to dominate your term of office. Some of them enjoyed the office so much that they don't want to give up the leadership role. If that is a problem, speak to them in private before meetings and ask for cooperation.

✔ **Set a time for telephone calls** unless you are available all day and all evening to accept them. You will be able to plan your time well when members are aware of your telephone hours. An answering machine is helpful.

✔ **Make lists.** This is part of "being prepared." If your meetings are local and at a regular date and time, your lists will be short. If your meetings are at a distance, especially where you will be staying overnight, your lists should include your packing list, your equipment list, your document list, and such others as you may require. As you pack, check off the items so that you won't forget something important. Lists have a calming effect.

✔ **Asking for help.** There will be times when you need help in one form or another. Many new presidents feel that the total responsibility for the organization falls on their shoulders and that they must go it alone. Not asking for help can have you in a stressful and often dangerous position. Do not be afraid or ashamed to ask for help when you need it. No one is expected to be all things to all members.

During the Meeting

✔ **You are the leader.** You are the leader of your organization. Your appearance of **impartiality** is the most important aspect of your position. You are leader of all members, even when they oppose you. In meetings, you must never favor one person over another in granting the floor for making motions or participating in debate. You want your reputation intact when you leave office.

✔ **Stand while you are chairing** a meeting of an assembly. You may sit if the meeting is of a small board, committee, or executive committee. You may sit when a committee or officer is reporting, then rise to take questions on the report. Ask the preparations committee to have an extra microphone for reporting members to use to avoid having them report from the station of the chair. During a meeting, only the president should occupy the station of the chair.

During banquets and other events that are not actual meetings, a single microphone may be used by all the speakers if there is not another available.

You should stand to call the meeting to order and anytime you are speaking from the chair. There are two symbols of authority in a meeting, the gavel and the station of the chair. The chair has greater authority when the chairman stands.

During a meeting, rising at critical times can be very effective in curtailing undesirable behavior. Occasionally a member will speak too long in debate, a committee chairman will take took long to make a simple report, or an invited speaker will speak much longer than he had been allotted. Standing can remind the speaker that there are other things to do.

✔ **Getting the meeting started.** Everyone is familiar with the group that stands around talking and doing personal business before a meeting. Obtaining the group's attention about one minute before the opening time of the meeting can save some frustration in starting. Go to the microphone and announce, "Please be seated." Repeat it until everyone is seated and ready to begin. That was the most helpful hint given to me when I first began to preside. If you start on time, everyone will know that they will miss something if they are late. If you repeatedly start late, members will start to come late. Your first meeting will set the tone for your administration.

✔ **Use of the gavel.** The gavel is used to call the meeting to order, and to maintain order during the meeting. Your gavel should be of substantial size. Baby gavels are not for serious presiding officers. Use the gavel with discretion. One rap should be sufficient to call the meeting to order. Repeated rapping only adds to the confusion. Wait until the members are settled down before rapping the gavel so that everyone is aware that the meeting is about to begin. See "please be seated" above.

✔ **Clinking a water glass for attention is a mistake**. It never fails that someone else will try to help out by also clinking a glass, then another and another. The others don't seem to notice anything but the music until the chair actually says something. If there has been a recess and members have filed back in, another method of getting attention is much better. I have a bell that I use in my *classes* to signal that recess is over. This is similar to the dimming of the lights in a theater to signal that the concert is about to continue. To get the members attention and to maintain order in a *meeting*, the only effective tool is the gavel.

✔ **When you serve as presiding officer**, you must remember that although you control the meeting, you are not the boss. The power of the Chair is in the office, not in the person. Such power is to be used to benefit the assembly in performing its duties and accomplishing its purposes. The fact that you are presiding gives you no more rights than the members in the assembly, and actually less. If you feel that you must take part in debate, then you must relinquish the chair to a vice president, and take your place in the assembly. You must remain out of the Chair until the pending question has been resolved. Then, and only then, may you resume the Chair. Avoid speaking in debate altogether if possible, especially in large meetings.

✔ **Being impartial** means several things. You must never become angry. You must never find a member's serious remarks or questions amusing. You must be pleasant, patient, and helpful. Your duty as chairman is to help the members by suggesting wording for motions when a member is having difficulty. The parliamentarian should be available to help members write their motions if necessary.

✔ **"Please" and "thank you."** When you start the meeting, and say "please be seated," is one of few times you will say *please*. We learn early in life that this is the "magic word" to encourage others to be more accommodating, and to stress in advance our gratitude. However, the meaning in meetings is different from other times. When you are introducing a report or taking the vote, you are enabling the members to fulfill their responsibilities and to exercise their rights. *Avoid* saying, "Those in favor, *please say aye.*" There are times for please and times not for please.

All elected and appointed persons are expected to do their jobs well. Saying "thank you" after reports is not necessary. A presiding officer thanking a person of lesser rank after a report, and not thanking the more well-known persons, is not uncommon. Sometimes, saying "Thank you" is actually an insult. Keep in mind that members are working for the organization and not for you personally as president. Save *thank you's* for the close of the meeting, when you thank everyone for their participation.

✔ **Appointments of special committees for the meeting** are made early in the meeting. Occasionally you will need a tellers committee or election committee, timer, doorkeeper, and others. Try to appoint different persons each time to these special committees so that many of the members have an opportunity to serve. Appointing a chairman of tellers early in the administration is efficient. That individual will recommend other members for the tellers committee for subsequent meetings. If you do this, appoint someone who is knowledgeable about elections. The additional members of the committee will have an opportunity to develop a new skill. When the board is small, ask members who are not board members to serve on various meeting committees. That will help to involve other members and to give them a stake in the meeting—encouraging participation, attendance, and cooperation.

✔ **Responding to debate.** *Don't.* Inexperienced presidents find it difficult to avoid "explaining" in response to some negative comment from a member in debate. Avoid responding to debate, positive or negative, at all costs. Say, "Is there any further debate (or discussion)?" You are the presider, not the explainer. If a member asks a question in debate, refer the question to another knowledgeable officer or member. If no question is asked, simply go on to the next person who wishes to debate. You should answer parliamentary questions. Consult with your parliamentarian if necessary, always remembering that the chairman rules, never the parliamentarian. If you know that a subject will come up that will be controversial and require answers, decide in advance which members will be called on to answer. If you want your opinion to be expressed, ask a friend in advance to do it, so that your impartiality while presiding will not be questioned. There is no disgrace in such preparation.

✔ **Take notes.** If you are one of those who cannot take notes while presiding, be sure to ask the secretary or a friend to make an extra tape recording of the meeting, so that you will have an immediate record. You will be able to answer questions after the meeting when called upon, and before the minutes are distributed. If you are ever in doubt about a subject of the minutes do not hesitate to call the recording secretary and ask.

✔ **Remarks.** Learn how to phrase your remarks while in the Chair so that no extra words are used. You must be careful to avoid any personal opinion from slipping into your speech. That is a matter of practice. When you have learned the proper language of the presiding officer you will have learned to avoid extra words. During meetings, when thanking individuals, thank them in the name of the organization. Write your personal thanks after the meeting. An exception is in your annual or final president's report to the annual meeting, when you thank all who have helped during your administration. Even then, avoid using "I." Use, "Your President."

✔ When the meeting includes elections, and you are a candidate for office yourself, **you may preside at the election meeting.** Elections are not peculiar to particular members, therefore the situation does not apply to the presiding officer alone. Some presidents are uncomfortable presiding when they are candidates, although doing so is perfectly legal, and occasionally is necessary as other officers may be candidates as well.

✔ **Reports.** Reports are given in the third-person singular. "Your president reports..." Accustom yourself early in your practicing to avoid saying "I."

✔ **Unruly members.** Occasionally in a meeting a member will become unruly. This happens for various reasons, but in any case unruly behavior is unacceptable. Read thoroughly the section in Robert's rules that discusses disciplinary matters so that you will know how far you may go in controlling the phenomenon. If a member must be expelled from a meeting, be careful how the expulsion is done so that assault charges cannot be justified.

Occasionally you may meet a member who is resentful because he does not know parliamentary procedure. Be patient with him and try to understand why he responds as he does. Explain that doing things correctly is important, so that matters of business will not be challenged later on and cause problems for the organization. Appeal to his loyalty to the organization. These members do come around, so don't be too disturbed about it. Knowing parliamentary procedure is your best defense.

Members sometimes have a copy of the 1915 edition of Robert's Rules, and will read a passage from it to support their assertions. If you are knowledgeable about procedure you will know that the earlier editions have been replaced by more modern texts. You will also know that when a short passage has been pulled out of the text, the remainder of the text in that section may explain more fully the procedure in question. That includes any exceptions which apply. Encourage members to use the most recent edition of Robert's rules.

Occasionally a member will think he is a "hero" for causing problems for boards and officers. He will soon learn that he is not a hero—just a member with a lack of good manners.

In meetings where the members have a financial interest, e.g., homeowners and condominium associations, some members are alert for any perceived slight to their rights, and can be negative in the approach to decisions of the board. With some groups a lack of trust begins when the board is elected and causes some members to hesitate to serve on the board because of it. Members must be helped to understand that the board is made up of neighbors who are volunteers and are not paid for their services to the association. If the board has functioned within the limitations of the bylaws, has not overstepped its power, and has worked for the association's best interest, the member complaints can be handled by explanation of the decisions.

Keep in mind that the board can be wrong. Full disclosure of financial dealings early in the meeting can help to reduce complaints. Once the disclosure is made fully, explanation is given in board or committee reports, and the board decision is clearly within the power of the board, the trust of the members is earned. If a member continues to complain after all other members are satisfied with the explanation, the time has come for him to either acquiesce or to make formal charges, instead of disrupting meetings with his discontent. The member's personal disagreement with the decision is insufficient cause for disrupting meetings. Formal charges must have proof of error or wrongdoing.

Good communication throughout the year can help to reduce tension.

✔ **In debate,** rotate between the pros and cons if possible. If several have spoken in the affirmative, ask if anyone wishes to speak in the negative on the motion. If debate continues too long, ask if anyone has anything new to add. Sometimes that will have a calming effect and no one else will want to debate.

✔ Above all else, you must **keep your self-control.** You will not be able to control a meeting if you cannot control yourself. When the presiding officer is emotional and nervous, the assembly senses the tension and responds to it— sometimes in a very negative way.

✔ **Debate must not precede a motion** in meetings larger than small committee meetings. If a member brings up a subject without a motion, request that the motion be made before discussion is begun. If the member does not know how to phrase the motion, the parliamentarian should be able to help. Many members do not know how to make motions properly. Do not allow "I so move," or "I make a motion to that effect." These phrases are not clear in meaning and the secretary must make sense of them. Require long or complicated motions to be in writing. That all the members know exactly what is before the assembly at any given time is important. Allowing such incomplete proposals only serves to confuse. And, after the meeting, when the member has had a chance to think over what he wanted to say, he could contend that the minutes are incorrect because he meant something else. When the vote is taken, everyone should understand exactly what is being voted on.

✔ **Sometimes a member will cite a rule to reinforce his argument** for or against a motion. When this happens and you do not immediately recognize the rule, require the member to state which document contains the rule, what page it is on, and if necessary ask him to produce the document. This requirement prevents a member from using nonexistent rules to support his argument.

✔ **Points of order.** Settle them quickly, making your ruling as soon as possible. If you need to consult the parliamentarian, do so quietly and quickly. If you rule that a point is not well taken and the member and a seconder appeal from the decision of the Chair, be calm. General Robert tells us that we should welcome an appeal, because there is no appeal from the decision of the assembly, and that we should be happy to have them make the decision. Sometimes an appeal is not easy to accept because it *feels* personal. It is not personal and you must accept it and handle it with calm and precise wording.

✔ **Place your gavel** on the table in front of you when you chair the executive committee or board meeting at a table when you will not be rising to chair the meeting. The gavel is a reminder that even though the meeting is less formal, the members have a chairman who is in charge. This will help to prevent a forceful member from attempting to monopolize the meeting.

✔ **Don't hurry through meetings.** Take your time to use the correct procedure. If you are chairing correctly the meeting will go more smoothly and will actually take less time than usual as matters are expedited with your new skills.

✔ **Always adjourn the meeting** by saying, "The meeting is adjourned." There are many very unwelcome things that can happen to presiding officers who habitually neglect to adjourn meetings. It could be that someone with a hidden agenda will take the chair and continue the meeting. If you don't adjourn it, the meeting is not officially adjourned.

✔ **Mistakes.** If you make a mistake while chairing a meeting, stop and correct the mistake and then go on. Trying to gloss over an error does not work because the error is noticed. A lack of correction is equally noted. Admitting and correcting a mistake leaves the listener with greater confidence in your ability.

✔ **Use your knowledge** for the good of the assembly. Some presiding officers are so eager to use their new knowledge that they want to show it off. If members do not understand a parliamentary phrase, explain the phrase or procedure and go on to the next business on the agenda.

✔ **Never "turn the meeting over"** to anyone. You must remain in control of the meeting, even when someone is giving a report or speaking in debate. You *do not* turn the meeting over to the committee chairman. Merely announce that the next business in order is the report of the committee. If for some reason you wish to leave the chair, say, "The president wishes to debate this question. The vice-president will please assume the chair." You must leave the station of the chair during this time and stand with the other members. When the subject of the debate has been disposed of, you may resume the chair and preside for the remainder of the meeting.

General

✔ **Minutes.** Some organizations take verbatim minutes. You would be wise to avoid verbatim minutes, unless your rules demand it, because all remarks are recorded. That may cause members to hesitate to express their opinions freely, and can lead to hard feelings. The meeting proceedings may be tape-recorded for use by the secretary in checking facts before typing the minutes. If complex or complicated matters are taped, the secretary should keep the tapes for several months in case a question arises that can be resolved by their use. Having a tape is useful when there has been a discipline problem that could lead to further complications.

For large meetings, a special committee may be appointed to approve the minutes. A minutes approval committee is especially efficient for annual meetings. When the association meets only once a year, that is too long to let the minutes go unapproved. If one of your monthly or quarterly meetings is designated as the annual meeting, the minutes may be approved at the next regular meeting. Your bylaws may provide that the board may approve the annual meeting minutes. Even then, a committee of three to correct them can save valuable time.

✔ **Board of directors meetings.** If you are the chairman of the board of directors, you may take part in discussion when the group is small. If the board is more than twelve, you should use formal procedure. Using formal parliamentary procedure is especially important when your group is incorporated. Your bylaws or other rules *may* state that the president *must* vote in board meetings, regardless of its size.

✔ **Chairing a committee meeting.** If you are a committee chairman, you may take part in debate, make motions, and vote. The rules for a committee meeting are much more informal than those for a board meeting or a membership meeting.

✔ **Always be alert** for problems, even when a meeting seems to be going well. Your instincts and intuition can help you when difficult or complex matters suddenly arise if you are alert for them. Of course you will know your parliamentary procedure well enough to handle it.

✔ **A good leader** is a good communicator. Following the business at hand, tending to details, and informing the assembly of the present course can save time in meetings. Always keep the assembly informed about what is being debated or voted on, and exactly where you are on the agenda. Phrases such as "The next business in order..." and "The question is on the motion that..." will help to keep everyone informed at all times.

✔ **Personality conflicts, intrigue.** Some members find intrigue to be irresistible. Added to that, personality conflicts occur in all organizations. There are always "factions" within any group. Avoid attaching yourself to any faction or certain group when intrigue begins. You must remain impartial in any conflict. Recognize that legitimate differences of opinion are not necessarily factions, and must be treated with fairness.

Personality conflicts can lead an undisciplined member to goad the presiding officer. Sometimes this is nothing more than persistent "points of order." If this happens frequently, announce during the meeting that points of order should be reserved for serious infractions of the rules and not for inconsequential matters. If the member makes obscure motions to test you, remain calm, check with your parliamentarian, handle the motion, and then go on with the meeting. The member who goads the chair loses credibility with the other members. Your calm handling of the situation is equally and favorably noted.

✔ *The reading desk or stand* with a slanted top to hold books and papers is the **lectern**. The **podium** is the *dais*, or *raised platform*, upon which the floor *lectern* stands. A table *lectern* is sometimes used. *The Chair stands on the podium and presides at the lectern.*

✔ Decide well before the meeting what **material you will bring to the lectern.** You are less likely to lose your wits if you organize well. You should have nothing more than your agenda on the surface of the lectern. A three-ring binder is helpful to keep all other papers in the proper order. Proper order does not mean by category— it means in order of introduction on the agenda. For example, if the next item of business is the report of the membership committee, you do not need the entire membership file in that place, just the papers required for that report. All extra material should be kept under the lectern on the table, on the lectern shelf, or on a nearby table. Having several folders and notebooks on the table in front of you can be overwhelming. You will not have time for searching.

✔ **Equipment.** Ensure that you will have all the equipment that you will need in the meeting room. That includes microphones, overhead projectors, and screens. If the room is large, a microphone for the presiding officer is necessary, and debate from the floor may be heard by all present if there is a microphone on the floor of the assembly. That will prevent the necessity of the presiding officer having to repeat any questions that are asked. Make certain that the equipment is in good working order. Appoint someone with skills in handling the equipment to stand by in case repairs or adjustments are needed.

✔ **Choose suitable meeting rooms.** Ask your meeting arrangements committee to take into consideration the anticipated attendance and plan for a few more than that. The meeting room setup by the hotel or conference center will be determined by your need for writing tables. Be sure that there will be no conflicting noise such as loud microphone speakers on the other side of the wall during your meeting. Some hotels plan for several organizations to meet at the same time, and that can cause conflict in the sound level.

✔ **A round table** for meetings promotes more interaction among participants. It also diminishes the authority of the chairman because the chair has no specific station. Place your gavel on the table in front of you to establish your authority. You can place a table lectern at your place, and rise to chair the meeting. This will help to make the meeting more formal, and to prevent disorder. Try to avoid round tables for formal meetings.

✔ **President's record keeping.** Keep a record for yourself of problems that occur in meetings. Review your record occasionally to spark ideas for solving similar problems. If you have a problem that repeatedly occurs, consult a professional parliamentarian.

The record of problems can be passed along to the next president to help prepare for chairing the organization's meetings. That is a great service to your organization, and you will be remembered as generous and helpful.

✔ **President's reports.** Give your report in the third person singular. "The president reports... .." or "Your president reports... ." Avoid passive voice, for example, "it was accomplished... ." Use active voice, for example, "The organization accomplished... ." Always give credit where credit is due.

✔ **A little psychology.** Always keep your hands on the table. When you are sitting at the head table, or among others at a small table for a meeting, never sit with your hands in your lap. Remember the adage 'under the table deals' and you will remember the psychology of keeping your hands above board. An added value of hands on the table is that everyone can see that you are always ready to use the gavel if necessary.

The Gavel

You can usually purchase gavels at trophy shops. The shops will also engrave the nameplate for you.

Gavels come in many sizes. The smallest are merely ornamental and should not be used for an actual meeting. These ornamental gavels are often presented in recognition of service. They can be made of porcelain, glass, wood, brass or anything the artist desires. They may be placed on commemorative plaques.

Useful gavels come in sizes for women and for men. The woman's gavel is smaller than the man's. I don't recommend the smaller gavel for anyone serious about presiding. In this era of enlightenment of such things, one would think that the gavel makers would adopt some other designation for the sizes. There is also a judge's gavel, my own preference. It is a good size, not too large, and makes a good "rap."

You may also wish to have a sounding block. These are usually round, but can be in any shape. Be careful with the sounding block. Use it only in large halls and away from the microphone.

If the organization owns a gavel that was presented to you at your installation, keep it in a safe place, so that you can find it to pass it on at the end of your term of office.

You may use the organization's gavel if you wish; if it is a ceremonial gavel, you must use it for the intended purpose.

If you are not required to use the organization's gavel, you may use your own. It is important for you to feel comfortable with it during meetings.

Among my collection of gavels are all sizes, and some are extraordinary–brass and carved wood. There are also some very, very small ones. Other than my regular presiding gavel, my favorites are three and four inch wood gavels awarded by Eva Dixon, PRP, of Jacksonville, Florida, who presents them as rewards to quick participants in her workshops.

Choose your gavel carefully; use it judiciously and with restraint.

Parliamentary Law
Parliamentary Law is the body of enacted rules
and recognized usages which govern
the procedure of deliberative assemblies.

•

Parliamentary Procedure
A logical procedure for the implementation of
parliamentary law in meetings.

•

Principles
Rule of the majority, right of the minority
to be heard,
equality of opinion, protection of absentees,
one subject at a time.

•

Purposes
Orderly conduct of business, protection of the
rights of members, solid foundation for
resolving questions
of procedure, decorum in debate.

Chapter Two

Duties of Officers, Directors, and Committees

When things get rough, remember:
It's the rubbing that brings out the shine. *Unknown.*

Officers

President

The bylaws will prescribe the duties of all officers. Other than the bylaws stipulations, the president is usually the presiding officer of all meetings—Board, Executive Committee, Membership, Annual. The president as presiding officer is required to:

• Call the meeting to order on time.

• Announce business according to the prescribed order of business.

• Recognize members who are entitled to the floor.

• State and put all questions that legitimately come before the assembly, and announce the result of the vote.

• Rule on points of order.

• Maintain order throughout the meeting.

• Enforce the rules of debate and decorum.

• Expedite business, and do so fairly.

• Answer parliamentary inquiries.

• Provide factual information in response to questions, without expressing opinion.

• Declare the meeting adjourned at the appropriate time.

The Chair should stand when calling the meeting to order, introducing business, and when stating and putting the question.

Vice President

The bylaws will specify the duties of the vice presidents. They may be required to serve as committee chairmen or perform other duties. Otherwise the vice presidents, in order of their listing in the bylaws, will be called upon to fulfill the duties of president when the president is absent. Performing the duties includes chairing meetings; it does not include appointment of committees listed by name in the bylaws, or performing ex officio duties ascribed by the bylaws to the president. A vice president may not exceed the powers given to him in the bylaws. When there are two or more vice presidents, they should be designated in the bylaws as *first, second, third.* If titles such as *vice president of membership* are used the bylaws should state which vice president shall fulfill the duties of president when the president is absent or is unable to continue in office.

President Elect

The president-elect has been elected president, the term of office to begin at the close of the current president's term. If the organization has a president-elect, there is no election for "president" as such unless the president-elect resigns before becoming president. The bylaws should provide for filling vacancies in the office of president-elect.

Unless the bylaws prescribe, the president-elect does not chair meetings in the absence of the president, or assume the presidency in the case of a vacancy. The bylaws usually provide that these duties and powers shall be ascribed to a vice president. The time when the president-elect becomes president remains the same as when he was elected. The bylaws may assign certain other duties to the president-elect.

Recording Secretary

When the term Secretary is used without qualification, it means the Recording Secretary, not the Corresponding Secretary if there is one. The Recording Secretary is responsible for recording the proceedings of the organization's meetings. The secretary is responsible for the accuracy of the minutes even when the minutes are recorded by a staff member or other person. In incorporated societies, the Secretary is responsible for affixing the seal to official documents.

"Respectfully submitted" should not precede the signature of the secretary on the minutes. The office of secretary is as important as any other office, and does not require such deference.

In the absence of the president and vice presidents, the secretary calls the meeting to order and proceeds to elect a chairman pro tem.

Corresponding Secretary

Duties are specified in the bylaws. The bylaws may say "The Corresponding Secretary shall perform such duties as assigned by the president or the board of directors," rather than specify individual duties.

Treasurer

The treasurer is responsible for the funds of the association. Usually that means record keeping, and presenting a financial report at regular and annual meetings. Sometimes the association bylaws prescribe that the treasurer shall be responsible for investing the funds or managing the association's investment portfolio.

The report of the treasurer at regular meetings or annual meetings *is not adopted or approved*. Frequently an error in typing or calculating will show up on the report of the treasurer and must be corrected in the next report. If the Treasurer's financial report is adopted, all errors are adopted with it. The *audit* of the financial records is adopted. If your organization appoints an auditing committee, the *auditing committee report* is adopted.

Directors

Directors are considered officers of the association. Their duties and powers are covered in the bylaws. Directors must be careful to avoid going beyond the powers given to them in the bylaws. Usually the Board of Directors (or Managers or Trustees) is responsible for the business of the association between membership meetings. Often the board is given the responsibility for managing all the business affairs of the association. Large board meetings use formal parliamentary procedure. For procedure in small boards, see page 39.

The large board of directors is considered a form of assembly. Some association boards are required to perform their duties according to certain procedures specified in state and federal laws. Examples are state codes for condominiums and federal laws for labor unions. The board must follow its rules carefully for voting and record keeping.

Committees

There are **Standing and Special Committees**. The bylaws should prescribe how the committees shall be appointed, and their terms of existence. If the bylaws or special rules of order provide for certain **standing committees**, there may be no others unless the bylaws provide for the appointment of them.

Standing Committees are those that continue from one administration to another and have special duties, such as the membership committee. The bylaws should list them in order, and the bylaws or standing rules should list their duties, responsibilities and powers.

Special committees are short-term committees appointed for a special purpose. When the purpose has been completed and the committee has made its final report, the committee ceases to exist. The bylaws should provide for the appointment of special committees. Special committees report to the body that appointed them.

For example, special committees appointed by the board report to the board; special committees such as the tellers or election committee, appointed by the president at a membership meeting, report to the membership.

Vacancies in committees are filled by the appointing power. If the president appoints special committees, the president has the power to fill vacancies and to replace members of the committees when necessary.

The assembly may appoint special committees with the motion to "Refer To A Committee." Such a motion may include the method of appointment, the number of members of the committee, special instructions to the committee, and when the committee shall report. If the president has the power to appoint committees, a motion may be made only to refer the matter to a committee, specifying the duties of the committee and when the committee shall report. The president then appoints the committee. Motions may also be referred to standing committees.

Committee meetings use an informal procedure. The chairman may make motions and vote, there is no limit on debate, and anyone who did not vote with the losing side may make the motion to reconsider the vote. All members of the committee who voted with the prevailing side must be present or have been notified, otherwise the motion to reconsider the vote requires a two-thirds vote instead of a majority.

Ad hoc, task force, research group. All such groups are committees. The bylaws will prescribe the committees' titles. If the bylaws say *special,* do not call them *ad hoc* or anything else except *special.* Remember the importance of words to the members' understanding of what is happening. If the committees are called something else, someone could interpret that they are outside the rules for usual committees. To avoid confusion, it is better to use the term "special committee" in the bylaws instead of other terms such as "ad hoc" or "task force."

Committees can be valuable to an association. Many duties may be divided among numerous individuals working in groups. The time used in committee meetings is time saved in regular meetings.

Duties of Officers in the Bylaws

Where the duties of the officers are listed in the bylaws, and these duties are of the nature of rules of order, these rules may be suspended. Ordinarily the bylaws cannot be suspended. However, where rules of order, such as the order of business and the duty of the president to preside, are included in the bylaws, these rules may be suspended by a two-thirds vote or by unanimous consent.

There may be times when the assembly needs to deviate from the prescribed order of business and sometimes the president and vice presidents may be absent. If the bylaws provision that the president shall preside at all meetings could not be suspended, there could be no meeting at all when these officers are absent.

The Parliamentarian

The parliamentarian should be knowledgeable in parliamentary procedure for all situations in which the meeting may find itself. The parliamentarian never rules on a question. That is the duty of the Chair. The parliamentarian speaks to the assembly only when requested, and that should be seldom. The presiding officer and the parliamentarian should work out in advance how the Chair will be advised during meetings, so that the consulting is as inconspicuous as possible.

The presiding officer consults with the parliamentarian in advance on any business that it is known will come before the meeting, so that problems can be handled smoothly. The parliamentarian should be alert during meetings for impending problems and advise the chairman in time for him to avoid them. Consultation with the parliamentarian is important before meetings where elections will be conducted or amendments to the bylaws will be considered.

The member parliamentarian should be willing to give up the right to vote during her term, just as the president does, except when the vote is by ballot. If the parliamentarian is not willing to do that, he should not serve in the position. The presiding officer must be impartial and always appear to be impartial. That can be impossible if the parliamentarian is not impartial also. If your association wishes to allow the parliamentarian to vote and to speak in debate, adopt a special rule of order which allows for it.

The presiding officer may take the advice of the parliamentarian or not. The Chair rules. The parliamentarian only advises.

The Professional Presider and the Professional Parliamentarian

The Professional Presider

Some organizations retain a professional presider as a matter of policy. The professional gives the president the opportunity to present opinions on the matters to come before the meeting without having to remain impartial. The professional, being an outsider, relieves the other officers from the responsibility of presiding in the absence of the president.

A professional presider should be retained when the members and officers are at odds on serious matters. A professional will not have an interest in the business of the association and will be able to chair without emotional involvement or bias toward one side or the other. My experience in this has been very positive for organizations in trouble.

If the duties of officers are listed in the bylaws, they are considered rules of order which may be suspended. If your organization intends to retain a professional for all meetings, put this provision in the bylaws.

When retaining the professional, ask about experience and qualifications. Some professional parliamentarians do not preside professionally. If you need someone to chair the meeting for you, you need someone who is experienced, and has all the qualities of a good presiding officer.

Seek a professional who is a Professional Registered Parliamentarian (PRP) certified by the National Association of Parliamentarians. Others who are qualified are Parliamentary Specialists from the Academy of Parliamentary Procedure and Law, and Certified Professional Parliamentarians from the American Institute of Parliamentarians.

Ask how long the professional has held certifications. Newly registered or certified parliamentarians are qualified to serve as consultants, not necessarily as presiders.

Professional Parliamentarian

The professional parliamentarian must be retained early enough in the meeting planning process to be able to help the president and officers with the agenda, and to advise on notices and other important matters. As stated above for the professional presider, the professional parliamentarian should have attained certifications. Inquire about this when you talk with him or her. The parliamentarian will require a copy of the bylaws, articles of incorporation, minutes of the previous meeting, and other documents as needed. Make an appointment to talk personally with the parliamentarian to discuss the intricacies of the meeting and your chairing personality, and have the professional attend the pre-meeting board of directors meeting. This information will be valuable in helping the parliamentarian to help you during the meeting. A professional parliamentarian will help you and your members hold a meeting where the procedure is correct, and time is saved when members understand that an expert is present and available for advice to the chair.

A professional parliamentarian should be retained for meetings such as annual meetings and conventions, and when there are many conflicts among members. A registered parliamentarian will be able to advise the organization on its rules, and to write bylaws amendments or resolutions when needed. Written opinions based on the organization's bylaws and parliamentary authority may be obtained from some professional parliamentarians. Some organizations retain a professional as election supervisor.

Employed Staff

Certain clerical and other duties may be assigned to employed staff during the meeting. That may include a stenographer to record the minutes. Regardless of who records the minutes, the Secretary remains responsible for their accuracy. That is true of any duty of officers and committees, including financial reports. The Treasurer remains responsible for their accuracy. The responsibility may not be delegated; the actual performance of the task may be.

Employed staff from your own organization will be of great help in planning the physical setup for meetings. Staff can also be of service in other areas such as registration, correspondence, and technical advice about the organization. These are valuable resources. Don't underestimate the value of the employed staff.

Content of Minutes

Kind of meeting
(regular, special, adjourned regular, adjourned special
annual, adjourned annual)

Name of the organization

Date, time, and place of meeting

Regular chairman and secretary present
or persons who substituted for them

Minutes of previous meeting were approved
or approved as corrected

All main motions and motions that bring
a subject again before the assembly

Wording of each motion as adopted or otherwise disposed of
(debated or amended before disposal)

How the motion was disposed of
(or disposed of temporarily, and if there were adhering motions)

Secondary motions not lost or withdrawn
(record only when needed for clarity)

All notices of motions

All points of order and appeals
(sustained or lost, and reason for ruling by Chair)

All counted votes

The fact of committee of the whole
or informal consideration

The hour of adjournment

Signature of secretary

Chapter Three

Meetings

The secret of success is to be ready for opportunity when it comes. *Disraeli*

Decorum

Decorum is simply good manners. Decency in behavior is essential to productive meetings of any size. Even in heated debate tempers remain cool and feelings will be spared when members are courteous, although formal.

The presiding officer is addressed as *Mr. or Madam Chairman* or *Mr.* or *Madam President.* One does not address the Chair by his or her name. The presiding officer refers to himself as *The Chair,* never *I.* When reporting on his activities in behalf of the organization the president may say *"Your President reports....."* The bylaws will state the titles of officers. That is the only legitimate source of titles other than as stated above.

A vice president while presiding is addressed as *Mr. or Madam President* unless the president is in the room. Then the title used is *Mr. or Madam Chairman.*

Members address their remarks through the Chair, not directly to each other. In debate the discussion is on the pending question and the maker of the motion is not mentioned by name. One may say "the member" without questioning his motives. Members do not speak until they have obtained the floor (been recognized by the Chair), except in small boards and committees, or on certain motions that do not require recognition.

The Chair usually addresses the member as 'the member' unless the member is presenting a report or has risen to be recognized. In large meetings, some organizations have the member state his name and affiliation before he begins his speech.

All remarks must be germane to the pending question.

Members should not complain after a meeting that "something was not done correctly." A member's duty is to raise a point of order at the time of the breach of order instead of complaining about it later.

Members should not disturb other members by talking among themselves or walking around the room after the meeting has begun. Members who arrive late to meetings should sit in the first available seat without disturbing the assembly.

The members' duty is to be in their seats at the time for the meeting to begin, and the Chair's duty is to call the meeting to order on time.

Meetings and Session

The terms **Meeting** and **Session** are occasionally used interchangeably. However, a session is *the complete course of the conduct of business or agenda.* A session may last several days and be made up of many meetings, or a single meeting may be a session. A convention of one day, or several days, is a session. For example, a legislature may be in "session" for several months, and hold more than a hundred meetings during that time. Adjourning a meeting does not end a session.

Regular meetings

Regular meetings are periodic business meetings held at a regular date and time for routine and usual business. Regular meetings are described as being held at least more than once a year. One of the regular meeting dates may be designated as the annual meeting, or an annual meeting may be held separately.

Special meetings

Special meetings are held at a different time from the regular meetings and are called according to the provisions of the bylaws. Observe carefully how the bylaws are written for special meetings and who may call them and how. Occasionally bylaws will provide that special meetings may be called only for certain purposes.

The required notice of, or call to, a special meeting will include the business to be brought to the meeting, and the exact wording of any motions that require notice if they are to be considered. Only business specified in the notice may be considered at the special meeting.

The minutes of the meeting should reflect that the meeting is a special meeting and that all bylaws requirements have been met.

Annual meetings

The annual meeting is usually the time for annual reports, elections, bylaws amendments, and resolutions. Most states require nonprofit corporations to hold annual meetings. Even if you think you know the bylaws well, read them again focusing on these important items. Check that the appointed or elected tellers committee has had proper instruction in counting and recording the ballots according to your bylaws and parliamentary authority. When the tellers committee is well trained in the proper procedure, there will be fewer problems during and after the election. Consult with your parliamentarian about any anticipated problems. Practice your presiding language for elections, bylaws amendments and resolutions. Bylaws amendments and resolutions are main motions. Review the rules relating to each, as well as the related secondary motions that may arise. The classes you took in parliamentary procedure will save you a lot of pain later on.

Remind all officers and committee chairmen that reports are given in the third person. For uniformity, a written form for reports may be drawn up according to your rules and used for all reports.

Meetings of Small Boards

Large boards use formal procedure, just as an assembly does. Small boards are not committees and do not use the procedure for committees. However, small boards with membership under twelve, may use a more relaxed procedure than a large board. For example, where the meeting is held at a board table, the members are not required to stand while speaking. Members are not required to obtain the floor before speaking, and seconds to motions are not generally required. There should be no limit on the number of times a member may speak in debate, unless the board has adopted a rule regarding limits of debate.

Informal discussion of a matter is allowed when no motion is pending. This informal discussion may lead up to a motion before it is formally presented.

The chairman of the board may speak in debate and make motions, and may vote on all questions.

It is always better to establish rules for meetings of the board than to have misunderstandings from one meeting to the next about the procedure. The board should adopt rules that are suitable for its own manner of operation.

Adjourned meetings

An adjourned meeting is one which was continued by the motion To Fix the Time to Which to Adjourn. The adjourned meeting is a continuation of a meeting which for some reason did not finish the business prescribed by the bylaws. Adjourned meetings are also those which are continued because of a lack of quorum at the original time and place of the call to meeting. When your proxies state that the proxy is valid for the meeting date and any continuations thereof, that means adjourned meetings.

An Executive Session is one where the meeting is closed and the business conducted in secret. All who are present at an executive session are bound by the rule of secrecy. A whole meeting, or a portion of a meeting, may be held in executive session.

Statutes may require that your organization's board meetings be open to all members, or that all meetings of your organization are subject to the "Sunshine Law" and must be open to the public as well. In these cases, executive session may not be used except as defined by statute.

Conventions of Delegates

Conventions require special planning, both for the meetings and personally. If the convention is to last several days, plan the program so that you will have time to rest. Sufficient rest is important, and will prove to be so when complex matters arise in meetings. You must be rested and ready for anything. Plan for some exercise every day. Physical discomfort can impede your ability to preside with confidence and alertness. Engage a professional parliamentarian to help with the planning and to serve during the convention meetings. The assurance that comes from knowing that expert help is at your elbow does wonders for your self-confidence and enjoyment of the convention.

The committees that must be appointed for a convention are credentials, rules, and program. Others, such as tellers (election committee), will be required. The membership of the convention and the voting strength to determine a quorum is the first item of business at a convention. Voting on nothing else can take place until it is determined who the voting members are. The credentials report is adopted by a majority vote. Standing rules for a convention are necessary to stay within the time limit. These consist of rules of debate, and administrative rules relating to credentials and election procedures. Standing rules for the convention are adopted by a two-thirds vote. The third item to be considered is adoption of the program. The program determines when various items of business will be taken up and may include times of day. The program will also include all other events of the convention. Adoption of the program requires a majority vote.

See example of Convention Standing Rules in Appendix IV, page 94.
See example of Annual meeting agenda in Appendix V, page 108.
See script for conventions in Appendix V, page 101.

Convention Committees

These committees are necessary for conventions. They will be helpful for annual meetings as well, especially if your organization is large.

Credentials Committee

The credentials committee verifies voting strength for the session. This committee may be involved in preparing, mailing, and verifying voting certificates and proxies. The committee reports when called upon by the Chair, immediately after the opening exercises. No other business may be considered until there is verification of the voting members of the convention and how many there are. The *roll of delegates* is adopted by a majority vote. The roll of delegates establishes the number of voting members and who they are. (For an annual meeting, the registration report is sufficient and is not adopted.)

Standing Rules Committee

The standing rules committee writes rules for administrative details of the convention as well as special rules of order for the meetings. The rules are adopted by a two-thirds vote.

Program Committee

The program committee compiles a program which includes all events of the convention and establishes days and times for them. The convention order of business is included in the program. The program is adopted by a majority vote.

Resolutions Committee

The resolutions committee functions according to the standing rules for the convention. Usually, resolutions are automatically referred to this committee for recommendations. The committee reports at the appropriate place on the agenda, usually as an item of new business. The committee makes recommendations on adoption of the referred resolutions, and may propose substitute resolutions or amendments to resolutions. The resolutions committee may originate resolutions on its own. Resolutions are Main Motions. If the rules do not require all resolutions to be automatically referred to the committee, then the committee is usually charged with writing a courtesy resolution of thanks for all who have participated in the event, or for thanks to a speaker or other dignitary.

Elections Committee

The elections committee or tellers committee will have been appointed to distribute, collect, and count the ballots, and to report the results to the meeting at the time called for by the chair. The chair then declares who is elected. The tellers committee may be called upon during meetings to count a rising vote in the assembly. The committee should also be prepared to take a ballot vote on any question when a motion is adopted to do so.

The preparation of ballots can be done by the tellers committee if the nominating committee has published the names of the nominees. The ballot should have the nominee's name first and a space after it to write in nominees from the floor if they are allowed. The committee should also have sufficient blank ballots on hand for second and third balloting in case the first ballot does not yield a majority on any nominee.

The tellers committee should have on hand enough blank ballots for several ballot counts on other questions. These should be blank pieces papers of the same size and color, and they may be printed in advance with places to write in the question to be voted on and places to mark "yes" or "no."

Order of Business

1. Call to order
2. Opening exercises
3. Reading and approval of the minutes
4. Report of officers, boards, and standing committees
5. Report of special committees
6. Special orders
7. Unfinished business and General Orders
8. New business
9. Announcements
10. Adjournment

How the Chair Handles the Order of Business

1. Call to order

With one rap of the gavel the Chair calls the meeting to order. "The meeting will come to order." "The Thirty-fourth annual meeting of the Bromeliad Society will come to order." The Chair's duty is to call the meeting to order on time.

2. Opening exercises

The invocation or prayer always precedes the Pledge of Allegiance to the Flag, after which any other opening exercises are in order. "Mary Brown will offer the invocation." "Please rise for the invocation and remain standing for the Presentation of Colors." "Please rise and face the flag for the Pledge of Allegiance to the Flag of the United States of America." "Please rise for the Pledge of Allegiance to the flag of our country." "Mrs. Barker will offer the thought for the day."

Roll call. "The Secretary will call the roll."

Appointments

"Without objection, the Chair appoints Mr. Jones, Mrs. Alpine, and Mrs. Rogers as Tellers. There is no objection and they are appointed." "Without objection, the Chair appoints tellers, ..." When the president has the power to appoint committees *without further approval*—"The Chair appoints... ."

3. Reading and approval of the minutes

Roberts Rules begins the order of business here. "The Secretary will read the minutes of the previous meeting." or "The Secretary will read the minutes of the (date) meeting." — "Are there any corrections to the minutes?"

Avoid redundancies such as "are there any corrections or additions." Anything done to the minutes at this time is simply a correction.
"The minutes are approved as read." or "Are there further corrections to the minutes?" *pause* "There are no further corrections and the minutes are approved as corrected."

Do not allow anyone to claim a correction to the minutes when an error was made in a report or a motion that was adopted. If the secretary recorded the report or the motion as it was made at the time, whether made incorrectly or not, the minutes are correct. The maker of the report or motion makes the correction at the next meeting, and the correction to the report is recorded in the minutes of that meeting. Errors in motions may be corrected by the motion "To Amend Something Previously Adopted." The minutes are an accurate record of what actually happened at the meeting. Correction of the minutes should not be a change of history.

The minutes are not the secretary's report. They are the history of the actions taken.

If the minutes have been published, the motion "To dispense with the reading of the minutes" is in order. However, do not dispense with the correction and approval of the minutes.

If a committee has been appointed to approve the minutes: "The committee to approve the minutes of the (date) meeting will report."

4. Reports of officers, boards, and standing committees

"The next business in order is **reports** of officers. Your president reports.. ." The officers and standing committees report in the order that they are listed in the bylaws. The treasurer's report goes here. "The next business in order is the report of the treasurer." — "Are there any questions on the treasurer's report?" — "The report will be filed." — The report of the treasurer is *not* approved or adopted. *Only the report of the auditor is adopted!*

Say "the next business in order." The next order of business means the next agenda, not the next business on the agenda. "Are there any questions on the report of the treasurer?" Use this as given. There is no need to ask if there are any corrections to the report of the treasurer. Who will know if there are any? "The report of the treasurer will be filed."

If the executive committee or the **board of directors** reports with recommendations: "The next business in order is the report of the Executive committee (or Board). The secretary (or chairman, if other than this meeting's presiding officer) will report."

The Secretary reads the report and says, "Madame President, I move the adoption of these recommendations." Board and committee motions do not require a second.

If there are several unrelated recommendations they should be considered and voted on separately.

"The question is on the motion that.... Are you ready for the question?" Debate takes place. "The Chair recognizes Mr. Smith." After debate - "The question is on the motion that.... Those in favor say *aye*. Those opposed say *no*. The ayes have it and the motion is adopted." Proceed to the next recommendation.

"The next business in order is reports of standing committees. Mrs. Andrews will report for the...committee." Standing committees report at the annual meeting and at other times when they have business to report. At times other than the annual meeting, ask in advance of the meeting if there is a report, and call on only those who are ready to report.

Continue as above for all standing committees, calling upon them in the order in which they are listed in the bylaws.

5. Reports of special committees

Only those scheduled to report should be called upon. "The next business in order is reports of special committees. The Chair recognizes the chairman of the Spring Fling Committee, Miss Adams."

Special committees report to the body that appointed them: Executive Committee, Board, Assembly.

6. Special orders

"At the (date) meeting the motion ... was made a special order for this meeting. The Chair recognizes Mr. Fortune."

Matters which the bylaws require to be considered at a particular meeting are also Special Orders, such as elections. A motion may be made a special order by a two-thirds vote to be taken up at a particular time. A special order is one which carries the stipulation that any rules, with a few exceptions, interfering with its consideration at a special time shall be suspended.

7. Unfinished business and General orders

The Chair does not ask for unfinished business. The Chair will know from the minutes whether something was postponed until this meeting. "At the September meeting consideration of the motion that ... was postponed to this meeting. Are you ready for the question?" *or* "Is there any discussion or any debate?" "Are you ready for the question?" is the expression used by the chair to ask for discussion and debate on debatable motions.

"Under Unfinished Business, there was a question pending at adjournment of the previous meeting. The question is on the motion "to purchase a new rug for the building entrance hall. Are you ready for the question?" *or* "Is there any discussion on the motion?"

Unfinished business: motions pending when the previous meeting adjourned, unfinished business not reached before adjournment of the previous meeting, and any general orders not reached before adjournment of the previous meeting. Never call this "old" business.

General orders: matters postponed, or made general orders at the previous meeting, to be considered at this meeting. Bylaws amendments are also general orders, and should be placed here on the agenda.

8. New Business

"Is there any new business?" "Is there further new business?" New business is brought to the floor by a main motion.

9. Announcements

"Are there any announcements?" If the Chair knows in advance of announcements, she may call on particular members to make them.

10. Adjournment

"If there is no objection and no further business, the meeting will be adjourned." (general consent) "There is no objection and no further business. The meeting is adjourned." or "The Chair declares the meeting adjourned."

If the rules prescribe an hour of adjournment– "It is nine o'clock, and the meeting is adjourned." *or* " The Chair declares the meeting adjourned."

If there is a motion to adjourn:

"It is moved and seconded to adjourn. As many as are in favor say *aye*. Those opposed, say *no*. The *ayes* have it and the meeting is adjourned."

At a convention of delegates: "The Chair declares the meeting adjourned *sine die* (pronounced sigh-nee dye)."

How to Complete Action on a Motion

1) The member rises, and addresses the Chair: "Mr. (or) Madam President."

2) The Chair recognizes the member (grants him the floor).

3) The member makes a motion: "I move that... ."

4) Another member seconds the motion.

5) The Chair *states the motion* and opens the floor for debate (on debatable motions). "It is moved and seconded that ... . Are you ready for the question?" or "Is there any debate?"

6) Members discuss the motion, after being granted the floor by the Chair.

7) After debate, the Chair repeats the motion and *"puts" the question* (takes the vote). "The question is on the motion that ... . "As many as are in favor say *aye*." *or* "Those in favor say *aye*. Those opposed, say *no*. The *ayes* have it and the motion is adopted (or *carried*)." Action on a motion is not complete until the Chair has announced the result of the vote.

Note: When a committee reports, the reporting member moves the adoption of any recommendations contained in the report. Committee motions and resolutions do not require a second.

In small boards and committees a second is not required.

Quorum

The *quorum* is the minimum number of members who must be present in order that business may be legally transacted. If the bylaws do not specify otherwise, a quorum is a majority of the members. An organization can set its own quorum in the bylaws.

When there is no quorum, the only business that may be transacted is:

1. Fix the time to which to adjourn
2. Recess
3 Adjourn
4. Take measures to obtain a quorum.

Quorum should not be confused with the term *majority* as used in voting. A majority *vote* is a majority of those *present and voting, not* a majority of those present, and *not* a majority of the quorum.

For example: If a quorum is 25, and there are 30 present, it is possible that only 16 members will choose to vote on a motion. In that case, the majority *vote* is more than half the votes cast, or 9 (a majority of 16, those voting).

If emergency action must be taken in the absence of a quorum, the president must take the matter to the next regular meeting to be ratified.

Seconding

A second merely suggests that the seconder believes that the subject should be discussed. Seconding a motion not suggest that the seconder agrees with the motion. If a motion has been stated by the Chair and debate has begun, the lack of a second is ignored. By debating the question, others have agreed that the motion should be discussed. If a motion which requires a second is adopted but has not been seconded, the motion **is** a legally adopted motion.

A motion never dies for lack of a second. The motion is merely not before the assembly for consideration. The maker of the motion may make the motion again later after he has recruited a second.

Precedence of Rules

Corporate Charter
(Articles of Incorporation)

Constitution

Bylaws

Special Rules of Order

Parliamentary Authority

Standing Rules

Don't Be Afraid
to make adjustments

during a meeting or convention. For example, if something in the meeting hall seems difficult to use, have it adjusted during a recess.

I chaired a very large convention where appointees were stationed at microphones throughout the hall. They would hold up signs as a member came to speak. This was intended to inform the chair whether the member should be recognized next or later at a specific time. There was a red sign for privileged and incidental motions, a green sign for main motions, a blue sign for subsidiary motions, and a sign that was orange on one side and white on the other to designate pro and con for debate. The lights in the back of the hall were very dim, and it was difficult to distinguish between red and orange and green and blue at such a distance. Before the first recess, while still at the microphone, I requested that those stations be moved up about five rows to made the signs more visible. This was accomplished during the recess, and the remainder of the meeting went well.

Committee of the Whole

The motion to refer a matter to a committee has three variations. Other than the use in a meeting to send a matter to a committee appointed by the president to research and report at a future meeting, a committee may be formed consisting of the entire assembly during the meeting.

The three variations are committee of the whole, quasi committee of the whole, and informal consideration.

Informal consideration can be used effectively in small assemblies where a matter can be discussed without the usual rules restraints on the number of times a member may speak in debate and for how long. The regular presiding officer remains in the chair, and any votes that are taken are final.

Quasi committee of the whole is best suited to medium sized groups. The regular presiding officer remains in the chair. The results of the committee are reported to the assembly for final consideration. When the quasi committee of the whole "rises and reports" the assembly is back to its regular rules of debate.

Committee of the whole is best used in large assemblies. The regular presiding officer appoints a committee chairman who chairs the committee of the whole. When the committee "rises and reports" the regular presiding officer resumes the chair and the appointed chairman reports to the assembly the results of the committee, and moves adoption of any recommendations. The matter is then handled as it would be in any other situation where a committee reports.

These devices are useful when there is a need for more freedom in debate than that allowed under the regular rules of debate for formal assemblies. These should not be used to delay business, but are sometimes useful. While the motion to go into committee of the whole is pending, time limits may be imposed on how long members may speak in debate and at what time the committee will rise and report. If limits are not imposed before the committee begins deliberations, no limits can be set by the committee itself.

The presiding officer should know how to handle these devices when a motion is made to utilize them.

Committee Reports

- Reports are written in the third person.

- The reporting member of the committee, usually the chairman, reads the report and moves the adoption of any recommended actions contained in the report.

- Committee reports consist of name, the facts found, recommendations, and signatures.

- A written report is signed by all committee members concurring, with the chairman's signature first, or, if signed by only the chairman, he writes "chairman" after his signature.

- "Respectfully submitted" is no longer used.

Introducing the Head Table

Of course we don't introduce the head table. We introduce the people seated there. Or should we? Perhaps instead, we should present them.

Whether to introduce or present depends upon whether they are known or unknown to the audience. If they are already known, they have already been introduced. Thereafter, they are presented.

The same is true of introducing or presenting the speaker at dinner or at an educational event.

What if some are known, such as officers, and some are unknown, such as visiting dignitaries? Some are presented and some are introduced. For example, if the state president is visiting a unit during the meeting in the morning, and the local members have not met her, she is introduced. If she is present at luncheon the same day, she is presented.

If a dignitary or other special guest is introduced at the first meeting of the convention, thereafter she is presented.

At the head table, for example: "The president is pleased to present those seated at the head table—Mary Johns, Recording Secretary; Ann Tolkein, Treasurer; Martha Harvey, Vice President, and Shirley Addams, President-elect. The president is very pleased to introduce our special guest who has taken time from her busy schedule to be with us this morning, our State President, Jane Orson."

The visiting dignitary with the highest rank is seated to the immediate right of the local president. Others are seated according to rank, or according to the offices they hold.

We shouldn't *introduce* those who are known to the assembly, but we should *introduce* those who are not. Those who are known are *presented.*

Voting

Chapter Four

A good example has twice the value of good advice.

The following definitions assume that your bylaws do not define the vote required for particular decisions.

The **usual method of voting** is by voice (vive voce). The Chair should always take the *aye* vote and the *no* vote, and announce the result of the vote. (Exception: The *no* vote is not usually taken on a courtesy resolution unless a member requests that the vote be taken.) Sometimes the vote is taken by a show of hands.

A member may vote against his motion—he may not speak against it.

Majority vote – *more than half the votes.*

This is sometimes wrongly interpreted to mean one more than half. More than half can mean counting the one-half that results from an uneven number of votes being cast. For example, if 31 vote, half is $15\frac{1}{2}$, therefore a majority is 16. In rare cases, when the bylaws permit, the vote is in fractions. Fractional voting sometimes takes place in delegations. When members may cast votes in fractions, as in the case where $15\frac{1}{2}$ is half of the votes cast, any fraction above $15\frac{1}{2}$ is a majority. "As many as are in favor of the motion say *aye*. Those opposed say *no*. The ayes have it and the motion is adopted."

Majority plus one

This is a form of the extraordinary majority. This is sometimes misinterpreted to mean one more than half. *You must first find the majority as explained above, and then add one.*

Extraordinary majority

This is any number more than a majority—as defined by your bylaws or other association rules. The term should not be used unless the bylaws define it. "The bylaws require an extraordinary majority of ... in the affirmative for adoption of this motion. Those in favor say *aye*. Those opposed, say *no*. The affirmative has it and the motion is adopted." "There is less than an extraordinary majority and the motion is defeated." When the bylaws are specific about the extraordinary majority, such as *majority plus 5*, then the vote must be counted.

Plurality – *the largest number of votes received.*

Usually this applies to an election or choice that involves more than two candidates or propositions. Your bylaws may prescribe that elections shall be by plurality vote. If plurality voting is to be used, the bylaws must authorize it. Otherwise elections are by majority vote.

Tie vote – *defeats the motion.*

(There is no majority.)

Exception: A tie vote sustains the decision of the Chair when there has been an appeal from the decision of the Chair. *See Appeal page 79.*

Two-thirds vote

This is at least two-thirds of the votes cast. A two-thirds vote is taken by rising unless the vote is by ballot. On motions which require a two-thirds vote such as bylaws amendments, when the vote is close, the vote should be counted and recorded in the minutes.

Language When the Vote is a Two-thirds Vote

"Those voting in the affirmative will rise. Be seated. Those voting in the negative will rise. Be seated. Those voting in the affirmative are two-thirds and the motion is adopted." *or* "There are less than two-thirds in the affirmative and the motion is lost."

"As many as are in favor of the motion will rise. Be seated. Those opposed will rise. Be seated. There are two-thirds in the affirmative and the motion is adopted." The best word is *adopted*. Other words sometimes used are *passed, carried* and *approved*. If you use *adopted* you will not be misunderstood.

or "There are less than two-thirds in the affirmative and the motion is lost." or *defeated*.

Note: A rising vote is taken on any two-thirds vote when the vote is not by ballot, and when there is a call for a *division of the assembly*. Counted votes, two-thirds <u>or</u> majority, should be taken by rising instead of show of hands if the group is of any appreciable size.

See Division of the Assembly and Motion to Count the Vote, page 79.

Division of the Assembly = Rising vote
Motion to Count the vote = Counted rising vote

Majority of the entire membership

This does not mean a majority *vote* of the entire membership—this means a *majority* of the entire membership. For example, if the entire membership is 300, the motion requires 151 votes in the affirmative regardless of how many actually voted.

Some bylaws require a majority of the membership for adoption of some motions. This is difficult to achieve, especially when the bylaws do not authorize mail or proxy voting. When the quorum is a majority of members, and rarely attendance exceeds the quorum, a nearly unanimous vote of those present would be required to achieve a majority of the membership. Bylaws should be written carefully to avoid such complications.

Some motions require two-thirds with notice or a majority of the membership. These are special cases, and the rule is there to protect absentees. (See Bring Back Motions and Incidental Main Motions.)

Majority Vote of the entire membership

All members must be notified of the pending vote and have an opportunity to vote.

Voice vote

"As many as are in favor say *aye*. Those opposed, say *no*." *or* "Those in favor say *aye*. Those opposed say *no*."

Rising vote

A rising vote is used in taking a two-thirds vote and in verifying a voice vote. A call for "Division" means Division of the Assembly (to take a rising vote to visually affirm the voice vote). A *Division* can be ordered by a single member without a second. The Chair must immediately take the rising vote. A rising vote in this case is not a counted vote unless the Chair decides to take a count. Sometimes, when the vote is close, taking a count is wise.

A motion from the floor "To count the vote" is an incidental motion that requires a second and a majority vote.

Chair: "Those in favor, say *aye*. Those opposed, say *no*. The *ayes* have it and the motion is adopted." Member: "Division!" or "I doubt the vote." Chair: "A division is demanded. Those in favor of the motion will rise. Be seated. Those opposed will rise. Be seated. The affirmative has it and the motion is adopted."

Chair: "It is moved and seconded to count the vote. Those in favor, say *aye*. Those opposed, say *no*. The *ayes* have it and the vote will be counted. Those in favor will rise and remain standing while the tellers count. (Wait for count) Be seated. Those opposed will rise and remain standing while the tellers count. (Wait for count) Be seated. There are forty-one in the affirmative and thirty nine in the negative. The affirmative has it and the motion is adopted."

Unanimous Vote

This means that there were no dissenting votes. It does not mean that everyone is in agreement, but that any dissenters did not vote at all.

Unanimous (or general) consent

"If there is no objection the action _____ will be taken." If no member objects, "Since there is no objection, the action is decided." If a member objects, "The question is on _____." Continue as if the motion had arisen in the usual manner.

Much time can be saved in meetings when routine matters can be decided by general consent. When there is not likely to be dissent, the Chair may use general consent in such matters as appointments (tellers, timers, and others) and allowing a member to conclude his remarks in debate when his allotted time has expired.

Unanimous consent is actually what takes place when the Chair says, "The Chair declares the minutes approved as read." Declaring the minutes approved is also an **assumed motion**. In some cases the Chair may "assume" unanimous consent. For example, approval of the minutes and adjournment may be assumed by the Chair without a formal motion. Even though there has been no formal motion, the action is valid unless there is an objection. In the case of an objection, the Chair states the question as if a motion had been formally made. "There is an objection. The question is on.... Those in favor, say *aye*. Those opposed, say *no*. The *ayes* have it, the motion is adopted and we will... ."

Absentee voting

Mail balloting is a form of absentee voting. So is voting by telephone or on-line computer. Your bylaws must allow for such voting if it is to take place.

Proxies are not votes in the real sense. They are powers of attorney for someone else to vote in the member's stead. The limited proxy which has preferences marked must be voted in the manner charged by the signer of the proxy. A general proxy gives the power to vote any choice to the proxy holder. State statutes vary regarding the bylaws requirements for proxy voting. Some states require that the bylaws must allow proxy voting if it is to be used. Others require that it must be expressly disallowed if it is not to be used. Check with your organization's attorney, or read the state statutes to determine which applies in your case.

Ballot voting

This is usually a secret ballot. A ballot may be used in voting on motions as well as on elections. In that case the member writes *yes* or *no* on a slip of paper supplied by the tellers. The motion to vote by ballot is an incidental motion that requires a second and a majority vote without debate.

If the bylaws require a ballot on elections, no other method is legal, even when there is only one candidate for an office. The motion "to have the secretary cast the ballot" *is not valid* and cannot replace the voting by ballot.

When the bylaws require a ballot on any proposition, and if the question is known in advance, the ballot may be printed.

Tellers must be instructed in the proper methods of counting and recording the ballots according to the bylaws and the parliamentary authority.

The Chair instructs the assembly on how to mark and fold the ballot or asks the chairman of tellers to do so.

"The tellers will distribute the ballots." After time has been allotted for marking the ballots, "Have all voted who wish to vote?" That ensures that all ballots have been collected. "If no one else wishes to vote, the polls will be closed. The Chair declares the polls closed. *or* The polls are closed." "The tellers will retire to count the ballots."

When there is a motion to close the polls, the required vote is two-thirds. To reopen the polls requires a majority vote.

A ballot is not necessarily always a secret vote. For example, if the board is allowed by the bylaws to vote by mail, any action which could have been taken in a meeting without a secret vote may be voted on by mail ballot. That is not a case for a secret ballot, unless it is the practice of the organization to have it so. Political parties use signed ballots in election of party chairmen and officers.

When a ballot is not required

In elections which do not require a ballot, a voice vote may elect. *When there is more than one candidate or choice on a voice vote, the first to receive a majority is elected, and the remaining choices are not voted on.* That is also true on motions which include a choice between several items. [The motion *To Create A Blank* is an example. The choices to fill the blank are voted on one at a time.] If the assembly is inexperienced in this kind of voting, the presiding officer should explain, before the vote is taken, that if a member has a preference he should vote *no* on the others. Because of some misunderstanding this kind of vote frequently must be retaken. The Chair can avoid that by explanation in advance of the voice vote.

Changing one's vote

On a voice vote, a member may change his vote *before the Chair announces the result of the vote*. Occasionally a member, usually on the losing side, will use this strategy in order that he may make the motion to *Reconsider*. One has to have voted on the prevailing side to move to reconsider.

When a voice vote is too close to call

The chair many retake a voice vote when the results are unclear. Sometimes when members become excited the aye vote or the no vote will seem louder than the other. The chair may retake the vote by voice or by rising, or he may require a counted vote. "The chair is in doubt about the result of the vote. The vote will be retaken. Those in favor, say *aye*. Those opposed, say *no*. The *ayes* have it and the motion is adopted." *or* "The chair is in doubt about the result of the vote. The vote will be retaken and counted. The tellers will count the votes. Those voting in favor of the motion will rise. Be seated. Those opposed will rise. Be seated. The affirmative has it and the motion is adopted.

Other Methods of Voting

There are numerous methods of voting. They include:

proxy

secret ballot

signed ballot

preferential

teleconference

bullet voting

cumulative voting

machine voting

Guide to Voting Procedures for Nonprofit Organizations is a comprehensive exposition of these methods and more. See last page order form.

Chapter Five

Language of the Presiding Officer

Even the simplest task requires the right sequence.

The following language for the presiding officer covers the most common items of business in meetings. A convention script which includes bylaws amendments and an election is provided on page 101 and a description and script for a bylaws revision is on page 111.

The scripts assume that motions have been seconded.

The script style will be interrupted here and there for additional explanations. For more expanded rules and situations, see *Basic Parliamentary Procedure Workbook* and *Robert's Rules of Order Newly Revised.*

Full explanation of all the rules is not possible here. However, many rules are contained in the script. Take notice when the script gives a majority or a two-thirds vote. Motions charts are provided in Appendix III. Refer to these charts as you study. The author uses *he* or *she* in the script, one or the other. She is not gender-biased, and she writes this way to avoid the he/she awkwardness.

No two presiding officers will do things exactly the same way. If you find your tongue tripping up on a phrase after much practice, use the other version.

Phrases used by the presiding officer:

When there is more than one way to say something correctly, both versions are given, one after another.

"It is moved and seconded that..." (*stating* the question)

"Are you ready for the question?"

"As many as are in favor, say *aye*. Those opposed say *no*."
    (*putting* the question)

"Those in favor, say *aye*. Those opposed, say *no*."

"The *ayes* have it and the motion is adopted." or *carried.*

"The *noes* have it and the motion is defeated." or *lost.*

"Those in favor of the motion will rise. Be seated. Those opposed will rise. Be seated."

"There are two-thirds in the affirmative and the motion is adopted."

"There are less than two-thirds in the affirmative and the motion is lost."
    or *defeated.*

"Those voting in the affirmative will rise. Be seated. Those voting in the negative will rise. Be seated. The affirmative has it and the motion is adopted."

"The next business in order is... ."

"The question is on the motion that... ."

"The question is on the adoption of the recommendation of the committee that... ."

"If there is no objection, ..."

"Since there is no objection, ..."

"Without objection, the Chair appoints... ."

"There is an objection. Those in favor of ... say *aye*. Those opposed, say *no*."

"State your point (of order)."

"State your question."

"The motion is not in order, as it is not germane to the pending question. The motion will be in order under new business."

"The next business in order is unfinished business. At the August meeting, the motion...was pending at adjournment. The question is on the motion that... . Are you ready for the question?"

First offence: "The member's remarks are out of order." Second offence: "The member will refrain from personal remarks. Personal remarks are out of order." Third offence: "The member will be seated!" Afterwards if offence continues: "The Chair has warned the member three times that his remarks are out of order, and he has persisted. The member will be seated or the assembly shall vote on the discipline to be rendered for the disruption of this meeting."

□ □ □

At this point you have learned how to *state* the question, "It is moved and seconded that...," ask for debate, "Are you ready for the question?", to *put* the question (take the vote), and announce the result of the vote. "The question is on the motion that.... As many as are in favor, say *aye*. Those opposed say *no*. The *ayes* have it and the motion is adopted."

When you have studied the rules and language for the main motion, the subsidiary motions, and the privileged motions, you will be well on your way to chairing a good meeting. Incidental motions are listed on the chart in Appendix III. Descriptions of incidental main motions are on page 84. All motions are stated and put the same way as the preceding motions. The difference in motions is how they are stated and put, what their purposes are, and which rules that apply to them. The companion book

Basic Parliamentary Procedure Workbook, or *Robert's Rules of Order Newly Revised* will give you all the additional information that you seek on these motions. Your study will be very rewarding.

When the Chair votes

The Chair may vote, if a member, when his vote will effect the result. Only in rare cases should the Chair influence the outcome. The Chair always votes when the vote is by ballot. The chair may not vote twice, as a member and again as presiding officer.

• "23 have voted in the affirmative, and 23 in the negative, and the Chair votes with the affirmative. Therefore, the affirmative has it and the motion is adopted."

• "23 have voted in the affirmative, and 22 in the negative, and the Chair votes with the negative. Therefore, there is a tie vote and the motion is lost."

• "9 have voted in the affirmative, and 5 in the negative. The Chair votes with the affirmative. There are two-thirds in the affirmative, and the motion is adopted."

When the President debates

"At this time, the President feels that his active participation in debate is necessary. The Vice President will assume the Chair." It is not prudent for the presiding officer to participate in debate. On occasion, however, when the President knows a great deal about a subject, although biased in his opinion on the issue, this is the language to use. The president may not resume the Chair until the question is disposed of in some way. If the motion on which the president debated is postponed definitely, the president must vacate the Chair when the question arises again for consideration.

During **nominations and elections,** the president may preside when he is a candidate because in an election any member may be nominated and elected. However, when there is a matter before the assembly that relates only to the president or presiding officer as an individual, that person must vacate the chair while the matter is debated and decided. When the matter has been decided, the president may resume the chair.

Another time that the presiding officer vacates the chair is during "committee of the whole." When the motion to go into committee of the whole is adopted, the president appoints a chairman for the committee. When the committee "rises and reports" the president resumes the chair to handle the committee report. See page 49.

Nominations (By Committee and from the floor)

Chair: "The next business in order is election of officers. The Nominating Committee will report. Mr. Plume."

Nominating Committee reporting member: "The Nominating Committee submits the following nominations:... ." No action is taken on the report, because the Chair will ask for nominations from the floor and an election will be held.
No second is required to nominations from the floor. Nominations are debatable.

Chair: "Mr. Currier is nominated for President. Are there any nominations from the floor for the office of President?" *pause* "Mr. Ives is nominated. Are there any further nominations for the office of President?" *pause* "Since there are no further nominations, the Chair declares nominations closed for the office of President."

A motion from the floor to close nominations requires a two-thirds vote for adoption. To reopen nominations requires a majority vote.

The Chair continues as above for all offices. Nominations may be closed after each office or when nominations are complete for all offices.

A person may be nominated for more than one office. If he is elected to more than one, if he is present, he chooses which office he will accept. If he is absent, the assembly should decide by vote which office he will fill, and then proceed to fill the other office.

Elections

Before ballots are distributed, the Chair instructs the members on how to mark the ballot, or, the Chair calls upon the chairman of tellers to instruct the members on marking and folding the ballot, and how the ballot shall be collected.

Chair: "The tellers will distribute the ballots." When all ballots have been distributed and time allowed for marking: "The tellers will collect the ballots." "Have all voted who wish to vote?" (to be certain that all marked ballots have been collected)

After the tellers have collected the ballots, including the Chair's (if a member): "The Chair declares the polls closed. The tellers will retire to count the ballots."

A motion from the floor to close the polls requires a two-thirds vote for adoption. To reopen the polls requires a majority vote.

Tellers return. The Chair calls upon the Chairman of tellers to read the Tellers Report. The tellers *do not* announce who is elected, they only read the tellers report.

Chair: "For the office of President: Number of votes cast, 36. Number necessary for election, 19. Mr. Currier received 28 votes. Mr. Ives received 8 votes. The Chair declares Mr. Currier elected President."

The Chair continues as above for all offices.

Balloting may be done separately for each office to be filled, or one ballot may be used for all offices.

Elections demand special care. The Tellers must be instructed carefully on handling, counting and recording the votes. Following is a sample Tellers, or Election Committee, Report. The chairman of tellers reads the report and hands it to the Chair, who then reads it again, office by office, and declares who is elected.

Example, Report of the Tellers
When there is a majority

Number of Votes Cast	558
Number necessary for election	280

For President

Mr. Jones received	281
Mrs. Alben received	176
Miss Bolin received	101

Example, Report of the Tellers
When there is no majority

Number of Votes Cast	558
Number necessary for election	280

For President

Mr. Jones received	279
Mrs. Alben received	178
Miss Bolin received	101

The candidate receiving the most votes is listed first, the candidate receiving the second greatest number of votes is listed second, and all others in the same way, regardless of the order in which they were listed on the ballot.

If the election requires a majority vote, and no candidate receives a majority on the first ballot, the Chair says, "No candidate having received a majority of the votes cast, the vote must be retaken. All candidates will remain on the ballot. The tellers will distribute the ballots." Continue as if no ballot had been taken.

If no candidate withdraws his name from the ballot, the ballot retains all candidates on all succeeding ballots. The balloting must be repeated until a candidate receives a majority of the votes cast.

Usual Methods of Nominating for Election

From the floor
By a committee

Usual Methods of Election

By ballot
By voice vote

Motions

When a motion is made and seconded, the Chair *states the question:* "It is moved and seconded that... ." You should never just proceed to "Is there any discussion?" without stating the question. As presiding officer it is your duty to keep the assembly informed at all times what question is before the assembly. It is your duty to see that the motions are stated in a way that the assembly always knows what is occurring in the meeting. Sometimes you must stop and describe "where we are" so that no one is confused. Always announce the *result* of the vote.

The following thirteen motions are called ranking motions. Each has a rank to each other. They include the Main motion, the Subsidiary motions and the Privileged motions. A motion of lower rank may not be made when a motion of higher rank is pending. The lowest ranking motion is the Main Motion, and the highest ranking motion is To Fix the Time to Which to Adjourn. The rank of the motions will tell you when a particular motion is in order. See chart in Appendix III for a visual representation of the relative rank of the thirteen motions and their rules.

Note [ ] indicates rules relating to the motion.

The Main Motion

An *Original Main Motion* brings a new subject for consideration.

An *Incidental Main Motion* relates to action of the assembly, and does not bring up a new subject. For example, To Amend The Bylaws is an incidental main motion. [Main motions are debatable, amendable, and require a second unless they originate in a committee or board.] The principle is that more than one person wishes the subject to be considered. Some incidental main motions require more than a majority vote. For example, To Amend The Bylaws, unless the bylaws provide the procedure, requires notice and two-thirds for adoption.

Member "I move that ... ."

Another member "Second." or "I second the motion."

Chair *states the question*: "It is moved and seconded that .... Are you ready for the question?"

Debate ensues.

Chair takes the vote: that is, *puts the question.*

"The question is on the motion that ... . As many as are in favor, say *aye*. Those opposed, say *no*. The *ayes* have it and the motion is adopted." or "The *negative* has it and the motion is lost."

Resolutions

1. A long or complicated motion should be in writing and may be in the form of a resolution. A resolution should be written in advance if possible.

2. A resolution may have two parts, the *preamble* and the *resolution*. There may be several preamble clauses and several resolving clauses in an elaborate resolution, or the resolution may be as simple as a motion, using the word *"Resolved"* instead of the words "I move." A preamble is not required.

3. Reasons for a *motion's* adoption should not be included in the motion itself. Members may agree with the proposed action but not with the reasons for the action and vote against it. And, reasons given within the body of an ordinary motion may be considered debate and would not be in order.

    The advantage of a preamble to a *resolution* is that a preamble states the reason for the resolution, but is considered separately. A preamble may be just a simple statement of background. When a resolution has a preamble, the preamble is not open to amendment until the resolving clauses have been debated and amended. The vote is then taken on the entire resolution, which includes the preamble.

4. The negative vote is not taken on a courtesy or complimentary resolution unless a member requests that the *no* vote be taken.

5. *A resolution is a main motion.* All rules relating to the main motion apply to a resolution.

6. An elaborate resolution contains several *preamble clauses* and several *resolving clauses*. Write each clause as a separate paragraph.

7. Begin each preamble paragraph with "Whereas" followed by a comma, and the next word begins with a capital letter. The preamble, even if it contains several paragraphs, should not contain a period. Close each preamble paragraph with a semicolon, followed by the word "and." Close the last preamble paragraph with a semicolon, after which a connecting phrase such as "therefore", or "therefore, be it" or "now, therefore, be it" may be used. When one of these phrases is used, no punctuation should follow it and it should be placed at the end of the preamble paragraph.

8. The word "Resolved" is underlined, printed in Italics or upper case letters, is followed by a comma and the word "That" which begins with a capital T. Begin each resolving paragraph this way or number them after the first "Resolved." Close each resolving paragraph with a semicolon, the next to last paragraph with a semicolon, followed by the word "and", and end the last resolving paragraph with a period.

Examples:

Resolved, That the Bird Watchers' League provide binoculars for each Junior member.

Whereas, Raffles are effective fund raisers for nonprofit organizations; and
Whereas, Currently raffles are unlawful in this state; therefore
Resolved, That this organization write to state legislators urging repeal of the law forbidding raffles;
Resolved, That the letters also urge that repeal of the law apply to nonprofit organizations only; and
Resolved, That this organization urge other nonprofit organizations to join us in this effort.

RESOLVED, That this organization_____;
2. That the letters_____;
3. That this organization_____.

"It is moved and seconded to adopt the resolution just read. Without objection, the resolution will be considered seriatim. The question is on the first paragraph of the resolution, "That… ." Are you ready for the question?" The paragraph may be debated and amended by a majority vote. Consider each paragraph separately.

The resolving clauses are considered first and then the preamble (whereas) clauses. After the resolution has been considered paragraph by paragraph, *the resolution, including the preamble and the resolving clauses, is voted on as a whole.* "The question is on the adoption of the resolution (as amended). Those in favor say *aye*. Those opposed say *no*. The *ayes* have it and the resolution is adopted."

Subsidiary, Privileged, and Incidental motions are called *SECONDARY MOTIONS.*

Subsidiary Motions

Subsidiary motions assist in disposing of the main motion in some way.

Postpone Indefinitely

[The motion is debatable, is *not* amendable, it requires a second, and it requires a majority vote.]

The purpose of this motion is to kill the pending motion for the duration of the session. The motion to *postpone indefinitely* opens the main motion to debate while *postpone indefinitely* is pending. If the motion to *postpone indefinitely* is adopted, the main motion that was postponed may not be brought up again at the same session: that is, at the same meeting or convention.

Member: "I move to postpone consideration of the motion indefinitely."

Chair: "It is moved and seconded to postpone consideration of the motion indefinitely. Are you ready for the question?"

Amend the Main Motion

(primary amendment)

Methods of amendment:

   To insert, or to add words at the end

   To strike out words

   To strike out and insert words,

      or to substitute (paragraphs)

[The motion is debatable, is amendable, it requires a second, and it requires a majority vote.]

The primary amendment must be germane to the main motion.

Member: "I move to amend the motion by inserting the word *plaid* before the word *wallpaper*." (primary amendment)

Chair: "It is moved and seconded to amend the main motion by inserting the word *plaid* before the word *wallpaper*. Are you ready for the question?"

Amend the Amendment
(secondary amendment)

[The motion is debatable, is *not* amendable, it requires a second, and it requires a majority vote.]

The secondary amendment must be germane to the primary amendment.

Member: "I move to amend the amendment by striking out the word *plaid* and inserting the word *blue*." (secondary amendment)

Chair: "It is moved and seconded to amend the amendment by striking out the word *plaid* and inserting the word *blue*. Are you ready for the question?"

Practice—Main Motion with an amendment and an amendment to the amendment:

"It is moved and seconded that 'the club purchase new furniture for the clubhouse lounge.' Are you ready for the question?" or, "Is there any discussion?"

"It is moved and seconded to *amend the motion* by inserting the word *wicker* before the word *furniture*. Is there any discussion?"

"The question is on the motion to amend the main motion by inserting the word *wicker* before the word *furniture*. Are you ready for the question?"

Member: "I move to *amend the amendment* by striking out the work *wicker* and inserting the word *rattan*."

Chair: "It is moved and seconded to amend the amendment by striking out the word *wicker* and inserting the word *rattan*. Are you ready for the question?" "As many as are in favor of amending the amendment by striking out the word *wicker* and inserting the word *rattan,* say *aye*. Those opposed, say *no*. The *ayes* have it and the amendment is adopted."

"The question is on the *amendment to the main motion* to insert the word *rattan* before the word *furniture*. Are you ready for the question?" After debate, take the vote. "The *ayes* have it and the amendment is adopted."

"The question is on the *amended motion* that 'the club purchase new rattan furniture for the clubhouse lounge'. Are you ready for the question?" The motion may be discussed further, and other parts of the motion may be amended. There can be no further amendment of the furniture material such as rattan because a third amendment is not in order.

Note: Motions are voted on in the reverse order that they were made. In the instance above, the final votes were: amendment to the amendment, the amendment, the amended main motion.

Amendment by Substitution

The motion to substitute is an amendment which means to strike out the whole motion and substitute another. The motion to substitute may be applied to any main motion, to a paragraph in a resolution, and to a paragraph in a proposed bylaw amendment. The proposed substitute must be germane just as all amendments must be germane.

To substitute is a *primary* amendment. While the motion to substitute is pending, the main motion may be amended (secondary amendment only) and the substitute may be amended (secondary amendment only). Then the vote is taken on whether to substitute. If the motion to substitute is adopted, the substitute becomes the *amended main motion*, and may only be amended further by adding words at the end. You will find the page on the motion to substitute in *Basic Parliamentary Procedure Workbook* to be helpful.

Refer to a Committee

The purpose of this motion is to put a pending question into the hands of a committee to consider, investigate, or to take action on certain matters, or to do all these things. A question may be referred to a special committee, or to a standing committee when the subject is within the standing committee's responsibilities. [Debate is limited to: the appropriateness of committing the main motion, instructions to the committee, and to which committee to refer the question. Amendment is limited to: another committee, adding instructions, and method of appointment of the committee. The motion requires a majority vote for adoption.]

Member: "I move to refer the question to a committee of three to be appointed by the president, to report at the next meeting."
Chair: "It is moved and seconded to refer the question to a committee of three to be appointed by the president, to report at the next meeting. Are you ready for the question?"

A motion is adopted, "To purchase a desk at a cost not to exceed $300, and to appoint a committee of three with full power to purchase the desk."

A committee with full power has the power to carry out its own decisions within the instructions given to the committee by the motion to commit. In this case the committee would investigate the cost and value of desks, choose one and purchase it in the name of the organization at a price at or below $300.

Postpone to a Certain Time

[Debate on this motion is limited to the merits of postponement and the suitability of the time. Amendment is limited to time, and to make the question a special order. A question may not be postponed beyond the next regular meeting. To postpone to a certain time requires a second and a majority vote for adoption. To postpone and make the main question a special order requires a two-thirds vote.]

Member: "I move to postpone consideration of the motion until the next meeting." Chair: "It is moved and seconded to postpone consideration of the motion until the next meeting. Are you ready for the question?"

"I move to postpone consideration of the motion until four o'clock." Chair: "It is moved and seconded to postpone consideration of the question until four o'clock. Are you ready for the question?"

Member: "I move to postpone consideration of the motion to the next meeting and make it a special order." Chair: "It is moved and seconded to postpone consideration of the motion until the next meeting and make it a special order. Are you ready for the question?" The motion to make a special order requires a two-thirds vote. Debate must be confined to the merits of postponement and whether to make it a special order.

A motion may not be postponed beyond the next meeting, and only to the next meeting if the next meeting is no farther in the future than quarterly. Otherwise, the most advisable choice is to refer the motion to a committee to report at the next meeting with recommendations.

To Modify Debate

[The motion requires a second, it is *not debatable*, and it is amendable only as to time. The motion may be *amended* by a majority vote, but the motion must be *adopted* by a two-thirds vote.]

Adoption of the motion may extend or limit debate in the amount of time and how many times a member may speak in debate on a question. The motion may also limit the time a motion may be debated.

Member: "I move to limit debate on the pending motion to two minutes per person." Chair: "It is moved and seconded to limit debate on the motion to two minutes per person. Those in favor of limiting debate on the pending motion to two minutes per person will rise. Be seated. Those opposed will rise. Be seated. The affirmative has it, and debate on the motion is limited to two minutes per person."

Member: "I move that debate on the pending motion be limited to ten minutes." If adopted, it means that at the end of ten minutes debate must end and a vote shall be taken on the pending motion.

The motion to limit or to extend the limits of debate, when another motion is pending, is a *subsidiary motion* and is not debatable, and is amendable only to the extent of the time of limit or extension. When the motion is made when no question is pending, to modify debate for the duration of the meeting is an *incidental main motion* and as such is debatable, amendable, and may be reconsidered. Both the subsidiary motion and the incidental main motion require a two-thirds vote for adoption.

Subsidiary motion: "I move that debate on the pending motion be limited to ten minutes."

"It is moved and seconded that debate on the pending motion be limited to ten minutes. Are there any amendments? Those in favor of limiting debate on the pending motion to ten minutes will rise. Be seated. Those opposed will rise. Be seated. There are two-thirds in the affirmative, the motion is adopted, and debate on the pending motion will be limited to ten minutes. The Chair appoints Robert Bees as timer."

Incidental main motion: "I move that during debate on all motions in today's meeting, debate be limited to three minutes per speaker."

"It is moved and seconded that during debate on all motions in today's meeting, debate be limited to three minutes per speaker. Are you ready for the question?"

"It is moved and seconded to amend the motion by striking out 'three' and inserting "five". Are you ready for the question?"

"The question is on the motion to amend the main motion by striking out *three* and inserting *five*. Those in favor say *aye*. Those opposed say *no*. The *ayes* have it and the amendment is adopted." The amendment requires a majority vote.

"The question is on the adoption of the amended motion to limit debate on all motions in today's meeting to five minutes per speaker. Those in favor will rise. Be seated. Those opposed will rise. Be seated. There are less than two-thirds in the affirmative and the motion is defeated."

The subsidiary motion to modify limits of debate relates to a pending motion. The incidental main motion to modify limits of debate relates to the entire meeting. *See Incidental Main Motions, page 84.*

The Previous Question

[The motion requires a second, it is *not* debatable, it is *not* amendable, and it requires a two-thirds vote.]

The Previous Question is a motion to stop debate and amendment and to vote now. The motion calling for the previous question requires a second and a two-thirds vote .

Many of the members will not be familiar with the motion as stated. Many members will understand "Call the question." You may explain that "I move the previous question" is the correct motion and means the same thing.

Member: "I move the previous question."

Chair: "The previous question is moved on the motion(s) that.... . Those in favor of ordering the previous question will rise. Be seated. Those opposed will rise. Be seated. There are less than two-thirds in the affirmative and the previous question is lost. The question is on the pending motion that .... Are you ready for the question?" or "Is there any further discussion?"

Member: "I move the previous question."

Chair: "The previous question is moved on the pending motion that ... ." Those in favor of ordering the previous question will rise. Be seated. Those opposed will rise. Be seated. There are two-thirds voting in the affirmative and the previous question is ordered. The question is on the pending motion "that... ." Those in favor, say *aye*. Those opposed, say *no*. The *ayes* have it and the motion is adopted."

A member *calling out* "Question!" or "I move the Previous Question!", or "I Call the Question", *does not stop debate*. The Previous Question is a legitimate motion. The member must first rise and be recognized by the Chair and then make the motion. The motion must be seconded. Then the Chair puts the question to a vote, "Those in favor of ordering the previous question will rise. Be seated. Those opposed will rise. Be seated." If the previous question is adopted the president immediately takes the vote on the immediately pending question.

If adopted, the motion for the Previous Question stops all debate and prevents further amendment of the motion. *No member has the power to stop debate on his own by calling out 'Question!' in a meeting. That would be a violation of the rights of other members. That is a situation where inexperienced presiding officers can be intimidated if they are not knowledgeable in parliamentary procedure.*

Member: "I move the previous question *on all pending motions.*"

The Chair takes a rising vote to order the previous question on all pending motions. If the previous question is adopted the Chair immediately takes the vote on the immediately pending motion, and then on all other pending motions, in the reverse order of their introduction. That could include a main motion, an amendment, a motion to refer to a committee, and any others that are pending. The immediately pending question is the last motion made that has not been resolved.

When the previous question is ordered, debate and amendment are stopped on all motions as specified in the motion for the previous question.

Lay the Question on the Table

[The motion is *not* debatable, it is *not* amendable, and it requires a majority vote. It may not be qualified in any way.]

This motion is sometimes wrongly used to kill the pending motion. If that is the desire, then the motion *To Postpone Indefinitely* should be used. The purpose of the motion *To Lay the Question on the Table* is to lay a question aside temporarily to take up urgent business. A motion *To Take From the Table* may be made by any member, and if adopted the motion is again before the assembly for debate. The Chair should not allow the motion *To Lay On the Table* to be used to kill a motion on the floor. The motion to lay the question on the table is out of order in that case. The Chair may explain the purpose of the motion and suggest the correct procedure.

Always remember that Robert's rules is for ordinary assemblies, and Legislative rules are for the Legislature. Some people hear legislative procedure and try to use it in their meetings because they do not have enough knowledge to distinguish between the two. The Chair has the responsibility of bringing the assembly back to the proper procedure for the particular assembly.

Member: "I move to lay the question on the table."
Chair: "It is moved and seconded to lay the question on the table. Those in favor, say *aye*. Those opposed say *no*. The *ayes* have it and the question is laid on the table."
Later — Member: "I move to take from the table the motion that.... ." (Incidental motion; see Appendix III.)
Chair: "It is moved and seconded to take from the table the motion that...Those in favor say *aye*. Those opposed, say *no*. The *ayes* have it and the motion is taken from the table. The question is on the motion that... . Are you ready for the question?"

IS IT GERMANE?

Remarks on the pending question must be *germane.* An amendment must be germane to the motion it proposes to amend. To be germane is to involve the immediately pending question or to be related to the immediately pending subject in some way.

Example:

A main motion is pending that "the club purchase a gavel for the president." A member moves to "amend the motion by inserting the word 'mahogany' before the word 'gavel'." Debate must be confined to the immediately pending question, the amendment. Therefore, a member may not discuss the pros and cons of "purchase", as it is not germane to "mahogany". *After* the amendment has been disposed of and discussion returns to the main motion, a remark relating to "purchase" is in order, because "purchase" is germane to the immediately pending question, the main motion.

Privileged Motions

Motions are privileged when they are important enough to be made while another motion is pending. The following motions are the only privileged motions. If no motion is pending, some are main motions instead of privileged motions. See page 84 for an explanation of main motions that resemble privileged motions.

Call For the Orders of the Day

This motion is made for the purpose of returning to the adopted program or agenda when the time has arrived for a particular item, or when the assembly has ventured off the prepared agenda. [It is a demand from a single member and does not require a second. A two-thirds vote is required to *prevent* proceeding to the orders of the day.]
Member: "I call for the orders of the day."
Chair: "The orders of the day are called for. The next business in order is... ." The Chair returns to orders of the day at the proper place on the agenda. *The Orders of the Day* describes the agenda or program which has been published or has been adopted. The order of business is also the Orders of the Day.

Raise a Question of Privilege

[This motion does not require a second, it is not debatable or amendable, and no vote is taken on it unless there is a disagreement about the privilege itself or unless the member states it in the form of a motion. As a motion, all rules of the main motion apply to it.]
The motion raises a question of privilege having to do with the assembly. The Chair handles the motion immediately if the problem can be handled immediately. To *raise* the question is a privileged motion. The question itself, if it cannot be handled immediately by the Chair, has no more privilege than any other motion, and can be handled later. No vote is taken, unless there is a difference of opinion on the subject of the privilege. For example, if a member raises a question of privilege that the room is too cold, another might think that the room is too warm.

These motions involve the assembly, its comfort and safety, and even its continued existence. To *raise* a question is privileged, and the Chair will usually handle the question immediately. The motion does not require a second, it is not debatable and it is not amendable. If the question cannot be handled immediately, the chair will request the secretary to make a note of it, and take it up at another suitable time.

Member: "Mister President, the noise from the hallway prevents the members from hearing the speaker. May we ask the people in the hallway to move on?"

Chair: "Will the doorkeeper ask the people standing in the hallway to be a little quieter." (Close a window, open a window, speak louder so that those in the rear of the hall can hear, the hotel is on fire.)

Take a Recess

This motion is to take a short break in a meeting, usually for a few minutes, sometimes for longer. The motion does not adjourn a meeting—the members return after the time set in the motion to recess, continuing the meeting as specified in the motion.

[The motion is *not* debatable, it is amendable as to time, it requires a second, and it requires a majority vote.]

This motion is a privileged motion when a question is pending before the assembly. When there is no pending business, the motion is an incidental main motion; it is debatable, and amendable. Some incidental main motions resemble motions of other kinds, but must be made when no business is pending. *See page 84.*

Member: "I move that we recess for ten minutes."

Chair: "It is moved and seconded to recess for ten minutes. Are there any amendments? *pause* Those in favor say *aye*. Those opposed say *no*. The *ayes* have it and we are recessed for ten minutes."

Adjourn

[This motion is *not* debatable, it is *not* amendable, it requires a second and a majority vote.]

The privileged motion to adjourn may not be qualified in any way. If the motion to adjourn is qualified it is an incidental main motion, not a privileged motion. When the motion is adopted, the meeting is not adjourned until the Chair declares the meeting adjourned. There are some motions which can be made even after the motion to adjourn has been adopted. The Chair should always make clear when the meeting is adjourned by saying so.

Member: "I move to adjourn."

Chair: "It is moved and seconded to adjourn. Those in favor say *aye*. Those opposed say *no*. The *noes* have and we will not adjourn."

Chair: "It is moved and seconded to adjourn. Those in favor say *aye*. Those opposed, say *no*. The *ayes* have it and the motion to adjourn is adopted."

Necessary announcements may be made at this time.
"The Chair declares the meeting adjourned."

Fix the Time to Which to Adjourn

This is to fix a time to continue this meeting. Occasionally it is impossible to complete a meeting at which business prescribed by the bylaws must be taken up. That might include the annual meeting at which elections should take place, and for some reason the meeting must end before the election can be held. The motion To Fix the Time to Which to Adjourn can accomplish the purpose of continuing the meeting at a later time or date.

[The motion is *not* debatable, it is amendable as to time, it requires a second and a majority vote.]

Member: "I move that when we adjourn, we adjourn to meet at 12 noon next Friday." Chair: "It is moved and seconded that when we adjourn, we adjourn to meet at 12 noon next Friday. Those in favor say *aye*. Those opposed say *no*. The *ayes* have it and the motion is adopted."

The minutes will reflect that the meeting was adjourned to meet again at the declared time. The minutes will also reflect that the adjourned meeting was just that and not a regular meeting. (Minutes: The adjourned meeting of the society was called to order at 12 noon.)

Thirteen Ranking Motions in Order from Lowest Ranking to Highest Ranking

Main Motion

—

Postpone Indefinitely
Amend the Main Motion
Commit or Refer to a Committee
Postpone to a Certain Time
Modify Limits of Debate
Previous Question
Lay the Question on the Table

—

Call For the Orders of the Day
Raise a Question of Privilege
Recess
Adjourn
Fix The Time To Which To Adjourn

Incidental Motions

This class of motions deals with procedures arising out of: other pending motions, another motion or item of business. These motions are incidental to the business that is pending, have been pending, or will be pending. Incidental motions are voted on as they arise, and most are not debatable. Incidental motions, with the exception of *Division of the Question*, yield to privileged motions. Incidental motions have no rank among themselves.

Parliamentary Inquiry

[No second is required. The motion is not debatable, it is not amendable, and no vote is taken on it.] A member rises to ask a question on parliamentary procedure relating to the business of the assembly. For example: "Madam President, would it be in order at this time to … .?" or "Mr. chairman, what vote is required to adopt the pending motion? "

Point of Information

[No second is required. The motion is not debatable, it is not amendable, and no vote is taken on it.] A member rises to ask a question relating to the business of the assembly or a pending motion. "Mr. President, I rise for information." The Chair will say, "State your question." and the member asks his question. The question is directed to the Chair or to another member *through* the Chair, not directly from one member to another. Do not allow members to talk to each other or to ask each other questions in open debate. "The member will direct her remarks through the Chair."

Point of Order

[No second is required. The motion is not debatable, it is not amendable and no vote is taken unless the Chair decides to ask the assembly to decide the point.]
This motion should be used when there is a violation of the rules of order, bylaws, or laws of the land. The motion should not be used frivolously. A point of order should apply to serious infractions of the rules. A member who constantly raises points of order on minor points is a nuisance.

Example: "Mr. President, I rise to a point of order." Chair: "State your point of order." The member raises his point, referring to the parliamentary authority, bylaws or other rules. You will either say "Your point is well taken," and correct the procedure, or "Your point is not well taken," and explain why not. No other members may debate the point unless the Chair asks for information from the parliamentarian or other knowledgeable member. The Chair may submit the question to the assembly for a decision.

If you rule the point not well taken, and the member and a seconder believe otherwise, they may appeal from the decision of the Chair.

Appeal From the Decision of the Chair

[The motion requires a second, it is not amendable, and it is debatable unless the ruling being appealed relates to indecorum, rules of speaking, or when made when the pending motion is undebatable.] When the Chair has ruled on a point of order, any member with a seconder may *Appeal from the Decision of the Chair*. A tie vote on the motion sustains the decision of the Chair, and the Chair may vote to create the tie. A negative majority is required to reverse the ruling of the Chair.
"There is an appeal from the decision of the Chair." The Chair then states the situation and the reasons for his ruling. "Shall the decision of the Chair be sustained?" (That means the *decision* of the Chair, not the Chair.) "Those in favor of sustaining the Chair's decision, say *aye*. Those opposed to sustaining the decision, say *no*. The *ayes* have it and the decision of the Chair is sustained."

If the decision is not sustained, the Chair corrects the procedure that led to the appeal.

When the motion is debatable, no member may speak more than once, except the Presiding Officer who may speak first and last.

This motion should never be taken personally by the chair. It is always possible for the most experienced presiding officer to make a mistake. It is better to let the assembly decide the issue than to leave an impression that the chair refuses to acknowledge that fact.

Division of the Assembly

[The motion does not require a second, it is not debatable, it is not amendable, and no vote is taken because a division is a demand.] The motion may arise in the form of a member calling out "division," or "I doubt the vote." That means that the member is demanding a rising vote to visually verify a voice vote. That is a *demand* and does not require a second. The Chair must immediately take a rising vote. If a member wishes to have the vote counted, he may make the incidental motion, "I move that the vote be counted." That requires a second and a majority vote to adopt. "It is moved and seconded that the vote on the pending question be counted. Those in favor, say *aye*. Those opposed, say *no*. The *noes* have it and the vote will not be counted."

Division of the Question

[The motion requires a second, it is not debatable, it is amendable and a majority vote is required.] When a motion contains more than one part, each part capable of standing alone as a separate motion, a member may move *To Divide the Question.* That means that each part will be considered and voted on separately. "It is moved and seconded to divide the question. Those in favor say *aye.* Those opposed, say *no.* The *noes* have it and the question will not be divided."

Suspend the Rules of Order

[The motion requires a second, it is not debatable, it is not amendable, and it requires two-thirds vote.] This motion applies to rules of order: parliamentary authority, special rules of order, standing rules. It does not apply to the bylaws. The motion must state its specific purpose. "It is moved and seconded to suspend the rule that interferes with taking up the report of the Membership Committee. Those in favor of suspending the rule will rise. Be seated. Those opposed will rise. Be seated. There are two-thirds in the affirmative, and the rule is suspended. The next business in order is the report of the Membership Committee."

Consider by Paragraph (Seriatim)

[The motion requires a second, it is not debatable, it is amendable, and it requires a majority vote.] Long motions which include several paragraphs, such as resolutions or amendments to the bylaws, which cannot be separated, may be considered seriatim, that is, paragraph by paragraph. Each paragraph is debated and amended separately. Then the entire resolution or motion is put to a vote. A long and complex motion may be considered seriatim by unanimous or general consent. "If there is no objection, the motion will be considered seriatim. There is no objection. Is there any debate on paragraph number one, that … ?"

Create a Blank

[The motion requires a second, it is not debatable, it is amendable, and it requires majority vote.]
A motion may be made which includes a blank. "I move that we purchase a desk for the secretary at a cost not to exceed _____." or a motion may be made to create a blank in a main motion that is before the assembly. The motion is pending "To purchase a desk for the secretary at a cost not to exceed $300." Member: "I move to create a blank by striking out of the motion the amount $300."

The purpose of creating a blank is to enable the assembly to propose any number of options without being restricted to the rules of amendment, that is, more than two options. The amount struck out automatically becomes one of the proposals. (To see how the motion *to amend* is different, see pages 45-46)

"It is moved and seconded to create a blank by striking out $300. Those in favor, say aye. Those opposed say no. The ayes have it and a blank is created. How shall the blank be filled?" Members suggest amounts, no second is required. When the vote is taken on the options, the first to receive a majority fills the blank. "Those in favor of filling the blank with ___, say aye."

The order in which the Chair takes the vote is as follows:

Amounts of money: To *spend* money—highest amount first. To *sell* something—smallest amount first.

Names—in the order they were proposed.

Dates, places, or numbers—in the order of their probable acceptance, beginning with the least popular, or in the order that they were proposed.

It is important in filling blanks that the members understand that the first option to receive a majority is adopted, so they must vote *no* on all except their own choice.

After the blank is filled, the main motion must be put to a vote. "The question is on the motion to purchase a desk for the secretary at a cost not to exceed $350. Are you ready for the question?" If a motion is adopted which contains a blank, the blank should be filled before any other business is taken up.

Questions Relating to Voting and the Polls

[The motions require a second, they are not debatable, and they are not amendable.]
"It is moved and seconded to close the polls. Those in favor will rise. Be seated. Those opposed will rise. Be seated." (two-thirds vote)
"It is moved and seconded to reopen the polls. Those in favor say *aye*. Those opposed say *no*." (Majority vote)
"It is moved and seconded to take the vote on the pending motion by ballot." (Majority vote)
"It is moved and seconded to count the vote." (Majority vote)
"It is moved and seconded to vote on the pending motion by roll call." (Majority vote)

Motions Relating to Nominations

[The motions require a second, they are not debatable, and they are amendable.]
"It is moved and seconded to close nominations." (two-thirds vote)
"It is moved and seconded that nominations be (by the Chair, from the floor, by committee, by ballot, by mail) (Majority vote) The motion is in order when the bylaws do not prescribe the method of nominations.

Request to Withdraw a Motion

[The request is not debatable, it is not amendable, and it requires a majority vote.] The maker of the motion may withdraw his motion *before* the motion is stated by the Chair. *After* the motion has been stated by the Chair, the maker of the motion must request permission to withdraw his motion. Permission of the seconder is not required. This is usually done by general consent. If there is an objection to withdrawal, the Chair may put the question. "The question is on the request to withdraw the motion. Those in favor, say *aye*. Those opposed say *no*."

Bring Back Motions

Motions That Bring a Question Again Before the Assembly

Reconsider

[The motion requires a second, it is not amendable, and it is debatable if the motion to be reconsidered is debatable, and it requires a majority vote] An unclassified motion. The motion to *Reconsider the Vote* must be made by a member who voted on the prevailing side, affirmative *or* negative. The motion *to reconsider* is debatable if the motion to be reconsidered is debatable. The motion to *Reconsider the Vote* must be made on the same day as the motion to be reconsidered was made, and must be called up before the adjournment of the next regular meeting. This motion may be made after the motion to adjourn has been adopted, and the Chair has not yet declared the meeting adjourned.

Take From the Table

[A second is required. The motion is not debatable, it is not amendable, and requires a majority vote.] To *Take From the Table* a motion which was laid on the table earlier in the meeting. Anyone may make the motion, including the member who made the motion to lay the question on the table. "It is moved and seconded to take from the table the motion that... . Those in favor say *aye*. Those opposed say *no*."

Rescind

[The motion requires a second, it is debatable, it is amendable, and it requires a majority with notice, otherwise two-thirds or a majority of the entire membership.] This is *an Incidental Main Motion*. The motion to *Rescind* is used to repeal an action that the assembly has taken previously. A vote cannot be rescinded after action has been taken, such as the signing of a contract or a resignation that has been accepted. The unfulfilled portion of a motion may be rescinded. The motion requires a two-thirds vote, or a majority of the entire membership, or a majority vote with previous notice.

Discharge a Committee

[The motion requires a second, it is debatable, it is amendable, and the vote required is two-thirds or a majority if notice has been given.] The assembly takes a matter out of the hands of a committee before the committee has made a final report, and considers the subject which had been referred to the committee. The assembly cannot discharge a Standing Committee which is authorized by the bylaws, except by amending the bylaws.

Amend Something Previously Adopted

This is *an Incidental Main Motion.* It may be applied to main motions, bylaws, special rules of order, and minutes of previous meetings. The vote required for adoption is the same as *To Rescind,* except in the case of amendment of the bylaws, which is two-thirds *and* previous notice unless the bylaws specify otherwise.

What did he say?

Incidental Main Motions

Incidental Main Motions relate to the business of the assembly and do not introduce a new subject for consideration.

Incidental Main Motions resemble motions of other classes, but may be made only when no other business is pending.

1. **Incidental Main Motions which require a majority vote for adoption:**
   Adjourn, when *qualified*, such as, "I move that we adjourn at five o'clock.", or when no provision has been made for another meeting (such as the last meeting of a convention).
   Adopt a committee recommendation not relating to a referred motion.
   Fix the Time to Which to Adjourn, when no other business is pending.
   Prescribe the Method of Nominations, when no election is pending.
   Ratify emergency action taken at a meeting where there was no quorum.
   Recess, when no other business is pending.
   Suspend a standing rule for the duration of the session.

2. **Incidental Main Motions which require a two-thirds vote for adoption:**
   Limit Debate or limit the number of times a member may speak on a question, when no question is pending.

3. **Incidental Main Motions which require for adoption a vote of: majority with notice, or two-thirds, or a majority of the entire membership:**
   Amend Something Previously Adopted
   Postpone an *event* or action previously adopted.
   Rescind a previously adopted action.

4. **Incidental Main Motion which requires previous notice** and **two-thirds vote for adoption:**
   Amend the Bylaws.

5. The motion *"Objection to the consideration of the question"* cannot be applied to an Incidental Main Motion.

6. It is important to remember that Incidental Main Motions which resemble other classes of motions **are in order only when no other motions are pending.** As main motions, they require a second, are debatable, amendable, and with the exceptions noted above, require a majority vote for adoption.

Motions That are Out of Order

Motions that are absurd are out of order. *Point of Order* is out of order if used solely for the purpose of obstructing business. Other motions used for that purpose are out of order as well, such as *Division of the Assembly* when the voting result is quite clear.

Your must use your best judgment to determine when motions fall into this category. Some members who have not studied parliamentary procedure have learned from experience that inexperienced presiding officers can be intimidated by particular motions. An example is the member who calls out from his seat, *"I call the question!"* The *Previous Question* is a legitimate motion, although it is a motion, not a demand. The motion requires recognition by the Chair *before* it is made. You may ignore these calls from the floor, or you may explain the parliamentary rule relating to it.

Occasionally a member will shout "Point of Order!" when he only wants attention. In many situations, he will ask a question or he wishes to speak against the pending motion. Some members seem to believe that in order to say something negative, they must shout, "Point of Order." Explain patiently that *Point of Order* is reserved for transgressions of the rules, and that the member merely must rise and address the Chair to be recognized. You might say, when he has finished speaking, "There was no point of order. The member asked a question." *or* "The member rose to speak in debate." That will assure everyone that you have not ignored a legitimate point of order.

Often it is necessary to explain the purpose of motions. If you handle these questions courteously although firmly, the members will soon learn the correct procedure. Your goal in chairmanship is to expedite business, while being fair and courteous.

The following language is for the Chair to point out that a motion is out of order or debate is not germane, or that proper decorum has been breached.

"The motion is not in order at this time." "The motion is out of order."
"The member's remarks are out of order, as debate must be confined to the merits of the pending question."

The member's remarks are out of order, not the member.

"The member will confine his remarks to the merits of the pending question."
"Personal remarks are out of order."

All debate on a motion must be germane, that is, directly related to the substance of the pending motion.

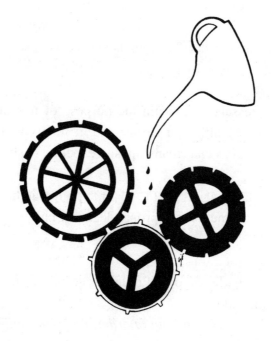

Good communication is the lubricating oil of organizations.
Some organizations require more oil than others.

Appendix I

SOME COMMON ERRORS TO AVOID

INCORRECT= NO		CORRECT = YES	
NO	"I make a motion"	YES	"I move that ..."
NO	"I want to make a motion."	YES	"I move that..."
NO	"I so move."	YES	"I move that..."
NO	"Question! Question!"	YES	"I move the previous question."
NO	"Mr. Black's statement is idiotic."	YES	"I rise to speak against (in favor of) the motion."
NO	"Jane, I move that..."	YES	"Madam President." (Wait for recognition.)
NO	Tellers declare who is elected.	YES	The Chair declares who is elected. (The teller merely reads the tellers report.)
NO	Introduce the head table.	YES	Introduce those <u>seated</u> at the head table.
NO	Old Business	YES	Unfinished Business
NO	"The next order of business is..."	YES	"The next business in order is.."
NO	"So ordered."	YES	"The motion is adopted."
NO	"Those in favor signify by saying *aye*." (redundant)	YES	"Those in favor, say *aye*."
NO	"Those opposed, same sign." ("Same sign" means that you are asking them to say *aye* when they mean *no*.)	YES	"Those opposed say *no*"
NO	"You are out of order."	YES	"The motion is out of order." "The motion is not in order."
NO	"Are there any corrections or additions to the minutes?" (redundant)	YES	"Are there any corrections to the minutes?"
NO	"Are there any corrections to the Treasurer's Report?"	YES	"Are there any <u>questions</u> on the Treasurer's Report?"
NO	"Do I hear a second?"	YES	"Is there a second to the motion?"
NO	"Do we have a motion to adjourn?"	YES	"If there is no further business, a motion to adjourn is in order." "If there is no objection, the meeting will be adjourned. Since there is no objection, the meeting is adjourned."

Appendix II

Glossary

Ad hoc committee • A special committee.

Address the chair • To speak to the presiding officer, using the appropriate title, and asking to be recognized by the Chair to make a motion or to speak in debate.

Adjourn • Adoption of this motion officially closes a meeting.

Adjourn sine die • To adjourn without providing for another meeting, usually at the end of a convention of delegates.

Adjourned meeting • A continuation of a regular or special meeting at a later date.

Adopt• A motion is adopted when the affirmative vote prevails. A motion is lost when the negative vote prevails.

Agenda• Program. List of items of business to come before the assembly. A list of things to do. Order of business which includes call to order and adjournment.

Alternate • A member appointed or elected to take the place of another, such as a convention delegate.

Amend • To change the wording of a motion.

Amendment • A motion which alters a pending motion. (Only two amendments may be pending at one time, a Primary amendment and a Secondary amendment.) To amend the bylaws is an incidental main motion.

Announcing the vote • A statement by the Chair giving the result of a vote. Action is not complete on a motion until the Chair has announced the result of the vote.

Articles of Incorporation • Corporate Charter. A certificate issued by the state under authority of law creating an entity which may own and sell property, sue and be sued, etc. The individual members of the corporation are not liable for the debts of the corporation. There are business corporations and not for profit corporations and, each will have statutes governing them.

Assembly • Members present at a meeting.

Aye vote • The affirmative vote.

Ballot• Usually a written vote. Usually a secret vote.

Board • Board of Directors, Trustees, Managers. A group of members elected to act for the organization as specified in the bylaws.

Bylaws • A document, adopted by the organization, containing the basic rules for governing the group.

Call to order • The official opening of a meeting.

Carried • The same as *adopted.*

Chair • The presiding officer, or the station from which he presides. Mr. Chairman, Madam Chairman. The presiding officer refers to himself as *the Chair.* Other terms which are used to describe the Chair, such as *Chairperson* are legal only when the bylaws so specify, and then are considered substandard.

Debatable • May be discussed. Some motions are not debatable.

Committee • One or more persons, appointed or elected, to investigate, report, or take action on particular subjects and questions. There are standing committees and special committees.

Constitution • A document containing the rules the organization has adopted for the management of its affairs.

Consideration • Discussion, debate, vote.

Consideration by committee • Discussion, debate, examination of referred matter.

Debate • Discussion following the Chair's stating a debatable motion.

Decision • A ruling by the Chair or by the assembly. The parliamentarian advises the Chair, the Chair rules.

Decorum • Appropriateness of conduct in meetings. Courtesy and decency towards other members during debate and conduct of business.

Division of the assembly • Call for a rising vote to visually verify a voice vote. This is not a motion for a count of the votes. If a count is desired, a motion to count the vote must be adopted.

Division of the question • A motion consisting of more than one part, each part capable of standing alone, may be divided, that is, debated and voted on separately.

In gross • Consideration as a whole. Opposite of seriatim.

Ex officio • By virtue of the office. The president is not a member ex officio of any committee unless such privilege has been granted in special rules or by the bylaws. Temporary officers do not assume ex officio duties.

Fix • In parliamentary terminology: to place definitely.

Floor, Obtaining the • A member is recognized by the Chair and granted the privilege of speaking.

General consent • May be called for by the Chair when there does not appear to be opposition to the question, or when there is no objection. Also called unanimous consent.

General orders • Questions postponed to a certain day or meeting. Bylaws amendments are General Orders as well.

Germane • Closely related, pertinent. All remarks must be germane to the subject being discussed. A primary amendment must be germane to the pending motion and a secondary amendment must be germane to the primary amendment.

Honorary • The title Honorary Member or Honorary Officer may be conferred upon a person only when the bylaws permit such a title.

Immediately pending question • The most recent motion introduced upon which no action has been taken.

Lost motion • A motion rejected by vote. A tie vote defeats a motion when a majority vote is required.

Main motion • A motion which brings a matter before the assembly for consideration and action.

Meeting • An assembly of members of a deliberative body to transact business or participate in a program.

Minutes • The official record of business transacted by an organization at each regular, special or annual meeting, or convention of delegates.

Motion • A proposal or proposition that the assembly take certain action or express itself as holding certain opinions.

Null and void • Having no legal effect. Invalid.

Order of business • The list of official business to come before the assembly, beginning with approval of the minutes and ending at the finish of new business.

Orders of the day • Usually the regular order of business, when classes of subjects are taken up in a particular order.

Out of order • Not in order. In violation of the rules of the organization or of the parliamentary authority adopted by the members.

Pending • Undecided or unresolved.

Pending question • A motion which has been stated by the Chair, and upon which no action has been taken.

Preamble • Introduction to a resolution. A preamble may be a brief statement of background.

Precedence • Established order of priority of motions. Rank.

Prevailing side • The side receiving the greatest number of votes. May be the affirmative side or the negative side.

Previous notice • As the bylaws or adopted rules of order specify. May be given at the previous meeting, by mail to all members, or in the call to meeting.

Pro tem • Pro tempore. Temporarily. For the time being. A member serving in the absence of the regular officer, chairman, or secretary is said to be serving pro tem.

Proxy • A power of attorney or written authorization for another member to act for another.

Putting the question • Taking the vote.

Question • The question is on adopting or rejecting the immediately pending motion.

Quorum • The *Quorum* is the minimum number of members who must be present in order that business may be legally transacted. If the bylaws do not specify otherwise, a quorum is a majority of the members.

Receive • Receive a report. The *hearing* of a report presented either in writing or orally. No action is required unless recommendations are included and moved. The reporting member moves the adoption of the *recommended* action. No motion is required to hear a report.

Resolution • A formal motion, which may include a preamble or not. A resolution should be in writing. Use the term *Resolved* instead of *move*.

Rules of order • Written parliamentary rules adopted by the members. Usually the parliamentary authority is a manual such as *Roberts Rules of Order Newly Revised*.

Second • Indicates that a second member is willing to consider a motion.

Secondary motions • Subsidiary, privileged, and incidental motions.

Seriatim • One after another in a series. To consider seriatim is to consider section by section or paragraph by paragraph. After all sections have been considered, one vote is taken on the entire document.

Session • A meeting, or series of connected meetings such as a convention.

Sine die • Without day. Used at the end of convention. *adjourn sine die.*

Speaker • The person who has been assigned the floor.

Special meeting • A meeting called between regular meetings for a special purpose. Notice must be given to all members of the time, place, and purpose of the special meeting. Only business specified in the notice may be transacted.

Special orders • A motion or subject assigned to a certain time, and made a special order by a two-thirds vote.

Special rules of order • Rules adopted by a two-thirds vote after notice, that modify the parliamentary authority.

Standing rules • Administrative rules that are usually of a semi-permanent or temporary nature.

Statutes • Laws enacted by state and local governments.

Sustain • Uphold the ruling of the Chair.

Tellers • Persons appointed or elected to count the votes and report to the assembly.

The special order for the meeting • A question for which an entire meeting is reserved. Questions to be taken up at a Special meeting for which notice have been given are The Special Orders for the meeting.

Vive voce • A voice vote.

Vote • The expression of the will of the assembly.

Majority vote - more than half the votes cast.

Plurality - the largest number of votes cast.

Two-thirds - at least two-thirds of the votes cast.

Tie vote - the same number of negative and affirmative votes.

Unanimous consent - no objection (also called General Consent)

Unanimous vote - no dissenting votes. This does not mean that everyone voted on the question, but that those on the losing side did not vote at all.

Yield • Accede to, relinquish. Motions yield to other motions of higher rank. A member may not yield any unexpired portion of his time in debate to another member. The right to the floor is not transferable.

Appendix III
Motion Charts

Motion	Second	Debatable	Amendable	Vote	Reconsider The Vote
RANK **Privileged Motions**					
Fix The Time To Which To Adjourn	Yes	No	Yes	Majority	No
Adjourn	Yes	No	No	Majority	No
Recess	Yes	No	Yes	Majority	No
Raise A Question Of Privilege	No	No	No	Chair rules	No
Call For The Orders Of The Day	No	No	No	Demand	No
RANK **Subsidiary Motions**					
Lay The Question On The Table	Yes	No	No	Majority	No
Previous Question	Yes	No	No	2/3	Yes
Modify Limits of Debate	Yes	No	Yes	2/3	Yes
Postpone To A Certain Time	Yes	Yes	Yes	Majority	Yes
Refer To A Committee	Yes	Yes	Yes	Majority	Yes
Amend The Main Motion	Yes	Yes	Yes	Majority	Yes
Postpone Indefinitely	Yes	Yes	No	Majority	Aff. only
RANK **Main Motion**					
Main Motion	Yes	Yes	Yes	Majority	Yes
Motions That Bring a Question Again Before The Assembly					
Take From the Table	Yes	No	No	Majority	No
Rescind Amend Something Previously Adopted Discharge A Committee	Yes	Yes	Yes	**	Neg. only
Reconsider	Yes	***	No	Majority	No

** Majority with notice or 2/3   *** Yes, if question to be reconsidered is.
Aff.= Affirmative
Neg.= Negative

Incidental Motions	Second	Debatable	Amendable	Vote	Reconsider The Vote
Appeal From The Decision of The Chair	Yes	1*	No	Neg. Maj.	Yes
Be Excused From A Duty	2*	Yes	Yes	Majority	Negative only
Call For A Separate Vote	No	No	No	Demand	No
Close Nominations	Yes	No	Yes	2/3	No
Close The Polls	Yes	No	Yes	2/3	No
Consider Seriatim	Yes	No	Yes	Majority	No
Count The Vote	Yes	No	Yes	Majority	No
Create A Blank	Yes	No	Yes	Majority	No
Divide The Assembly	No	No	No	Demand	No
Divide The Question	Yes	No	Yes	Majority	No
Method of Voting	Yes	No	Yes	Majority	Yes
Object To Consideration	No	No	No	**	Negative only
Point Of Order	No	No	No	***	No
Point of Information	No	No	No	No vote	No
Read A Paper	Yes	No	No	Majority	Yes
Reopen Nominations	Yes	No	Yes	Majority	Negative only
Reopen The Polls	Yes	No	Yes	Majority	Negative only
Request To Withdraw a Motion	3*	No	No	Majority	Negative only
Suspend Rules of Order	Yes	No	No	2/3	No
Suspend Standing Rules	Yes	No	No	Majority	No
Vote By Ballot	Yes	No	Yes	Majority	Yes

  * Page numbers for RONR: [1] 256, [2] 291, [3] 283

  ** 2/3 in the negative to prevent consideration

  *** Chair rules

Appendix IV
Examples

Convention Standing Rules

1. All persons shall be registered before being admitted to any business meeting.
2. Identification badges shall be worn at all times.
3. There shall be a designated seating area for delegates.
4. All resolutions, except those contained in the report of the Executive Board, shall be referred without debate to the resolutions committee to be presented with recommendations to the convention.
5. All main motions and amendments shall be sent to the Chair in writing and signed by the maker and the seconder.
6. Debate shall be limited to two minutes for each speaker and no speaker shall speak more than twice on the same question without permission of the assembly.
7. There shall be no smoking in the meeting hall.

Bylaws Article
Parliamentary Authority

The rules contained in the current edition of *Robert's Rules of Order New Revised* shall govern the Society in all cases to which they are applicable and in which they are not inconsistent with these bylaws, any special rules of order the Society may adopt, and any statutes applicable to this organization.

Note: The text of this article is from Roberts' Rules of Order Newly Revised, 1990 edition. For further details, see the bibliography.

Motion Form

Motion forms made up in advance and made available to members to use during the meeting will allow the secretary to keep track of the exact wording of motions. The chair will be able to state the question exactly as it was made. When the member knows he will have to write his motion, he will write it more clearly than he would if he just stood and said it.

The motions may be numbered for the secretary to have a record of what point in the meeting the motion was made. The secretary's notes may say only motion #1.. When the minutes are typed, the written motion is there for the precise wording and how the motion was disposed of. If there is any question later, the written motion is available.

Motion forms may be kept in a special file for reference.

Provide a carbon paper so that the member will have his own record. This can prevent disputes over exactly how the motion was worded.

Motion #_____   Date_____

I move that

                                                            _____

                                                            _____

Adopted ☐
Defeated ☐
Other_____

Deliberative Assemblies

Mass Meeting
(New organization)

Organized Society

Convention
(of delegates)

Legislative body

Board

●

Types of Meetings

Regular Meeting

Special Meeting

Adjourned Meeting

Annual Meeting

Executive Session

Examples for Ballots

> *Instructions on how to mark and fold the ballot should always be clearly explained to the voters before balloting begins.*

When the bylaws allow for only the nominating committees choices to be on the ballot, and when the bylaws prescribe a ballot vote, the ballot form is very simple and lists only those chosen names with places for check marks.

BALLOT

For President	☐	Morris Felinni
For Vice President	☐	Prudence Pedantica
For Secretary	☐	Gian T. Taller
For Treasurer	☐	Calvin Wimpie

When the bylaws allow for *nominations from the floor or nominations by write-in*, the ballot must provide a place for a name to be written in. When the ballots must be prepared in advance, the following example will be helpful.

BALLOT

Place a check mark beside the candidate of your choice for each office. Do not vote for more than one for each office.

For President

_____ Morris Felinni

_____ _____

For Vice President

_____ Prudence Pedantica

_____ _____

For Secretary

_____ Gian T. Taller

_____ _____

For Treasurer

_____ Calvin Wimpie

_____ _____

Secret Ballot by Mail

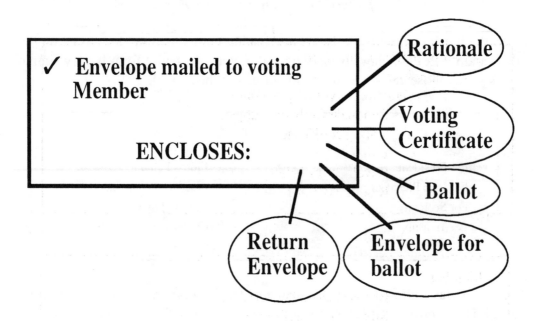

Return Envelope

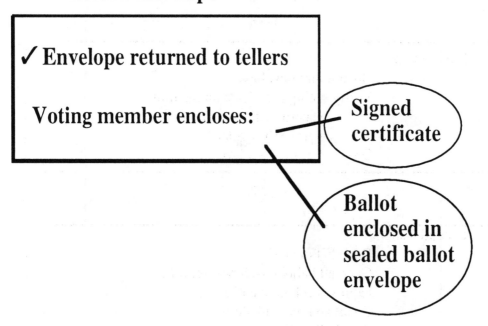

Mail Ballot
Counting and Recording Procedure

①

Envelope mailed to member:
    Encloses:
        Explanation of voting procedure
            Rationale for ballot subject
            Voting certificate
            Ballot
            Envelope for ballot
            Return envelope

②

Member:
            Reads enclosed material
            Signs voting certificate
            Marks ballot
                Encloses ballot in special
                envelope and seals it
            Mails ballot and voting certificate to
            tellers in return envelope

③

First Tellers:
            Open return envelope
            Verify voting certificate on the rolls
                Record that association
                member has voted
            Drop ballot in ballot box

④

Second Tellers:
            Open ballot box
            Open all ballot envelopes, remove
            ballots, stack in one pile
            Count and record ballots
            Sign Tellers Report

Appendix V

**Script for Chairing a Convention
with Elections and Bylaws Amendments**

Call to Order and Opening Exercises

Chair: "Please be seated."

Chair: "The Annual Convention of the Marcus Society will come to order."

Chair: "Chaplain Addams will lead us in the invocation and Janet Evans will lead the presentation of colors. Please rise for the invocation and remain standing for the presentation of colors."

Chair: "Please be seated."

Chair: "The welcome to Seattle will be extended by Jonathan Preston, President of the Seattle Chapter. Mr. Preston."

Chair: "The response will be given by First Vice President Ann Bradley. Mrs. Bradley."

Chair: "Your president is pleased to introduce Mary Alice Farraday, our opening speaker. Mary Alice is the author of *The Living History of the International Marcus Historians.* She has come to us from New York City where she lives with her husband and two teenage sons, and holds the position of Professor of History at the University of New York City. Mrs. Farraday."

Chair: "Thank you Mrs. Farraday for a very educational presentation. We are very pleased to have you with us here today."

Chair: "The meeting will be in recess for ten minutes to reseat the head table."

Recess

Business Meeting

The chaplain and the speaker will have left the head table, and the officers seated.

Chair: "Please be seated."
Chair: "The meeting will come to order."

Chair: "The president is pleased to present those seated at the head table. (See p. 50) Starting from the chair's far left, Charles Sands, Treasurer, James Whatley, Third Vice President, and Margaret Weldon, Parliamentarian. From the chair's far right, Janice Woodson, Second Vice President, Ann Bradley, First Vice President, and Jason Smith, Secretary."

Adoption of Convention Committee Reports

Chair: "The first business in order is adoption of the Report of the Credentials Committee. Nancy March, Chairman."

Credentials Committee Chairman: "Madam President, the Credentials Committee reports that registration as follows: Attached is the list of the names of the voting members of the convention and their alternates who have been registered up until 10:00 am. Delegates: 427; Officers and Standing Committee Chairmen: 21, Alternates: 210, with a total entitled to vote of 448. On behalf of the committee, I move that the roll of the voting members just submitted be the official roll of the voting members of the convention."

Chair: "Are there any questions on the report?"
Chair: "The question is on the adoption of the Report of the Credentials Committee. Those in favor say aye. Those opposed say no. The ayes have it and the report is adopted."

Chair: "The next business in order is the report of the Convention Rules Committee. Jason Anderson, Chairman."

Convention Rules Committee Chairman: "By direction of the Convention Rules Committee, I move the adoption of the Convention Standing Rules as follows:
Page 10 in the printed program.
1. Meetings shall be called promptly and delegates shall be seated before the time set for the opening of each meeting.
2. Members, delegates, and guests shall register before being admitted to the assembly hall, and shall be seated in designated areas.
3. Members shall wear identification badges at business meetings and workshops.
4. Non members of the association shall be admitted to the meetings only by consent of the assembly.
5. A member addressing the chair shall rise, give his name and the name of his chapter or other status.
6. Main motions and amendments shall be written, signed, and sent immediately to the recording secretary.
7. No member may speak more than twice nor more than two (2) minutes on the same question on the same day without consent of the assembly. Debate on any question shall be limited to not more than ten (10) minutes.
8. Non-delegates shall not be permitted to speak with the consent of the assembly granted by a two-thirds (2/3) vote without debate.
9. The pages will carry messages and deliver communications.
10. Tape and video recorders shall not be permitted in the meeting hall nor seminar rooms except those which have been officially assigned to record this convention.

Chair: "The question is on the adoption of the Convention Standing Rules as read. Are you ready for the question? (or, Is there any discussion?)"

NOTE: Any rule may now be amended by a majority vote. Any single member may demand a separate vote on any rule and it must be done.

Chair: "Adoption of the rules requires a two-thirds vote in the affirmative. Those in favor of adopting the rules, will rise. Be seated. Those opposed will rise. Be seated. There are two-thirds voting in the affirmative and the Convention Standing Rules are adopted."

Chair: "The next business in order is adoption of the convention program. Chairman of the Program Committee, Jeanette Martin."

Program Committee Chairman: "Please turn to page 7 in the printed program, schedule of speakers. At the luncheon on Saturday, the speaker will be Charles Mason, County Commissioner, to replace Shirley Mason. Madam President, on behalf of the committee, I move the adoption of the program with the change just made."

Chair: "The question is on adoption of the program with the change just made. Is there any discussion?"
Chair: "Those in favor of adoption of the program, say aye. Those opposed, say no. The ayes have it and the Convention Program is adopted."

"The secretary will report on the minutes of the previous convention."

Secretary: "The minutes of the previous convention were approved by the board of directors as required by the bylaws."

Reports of Officers

Chair: "The next business in order is reports of officers."

Chair: "Your president reports that ...."

Chair: "The First Vice President will report."

Chair: "The Second Vice President will report"

Chair: "The Third Vice President will report."

Chair: "The Secretary will report." *Note:* The minutes are not the secretary's report.

Chair: "The Treasurer will report."

Note: The treasurer's report should cover the period of time since the previous convention. The report is not adopted.

Treasurer: "The Treasurer's books were audited in July of this year. As provided by the bylaws, the audit was adopted by the board of directors. A copy of the audit is available for members at the registration desk."

Reports of Standing Committees

Chair: "The next business in order is reports of standing committees. If there is no objection, the Bylaws Committee will report last. There is no objection and the Bylaws Committee will report last."

NOTE: Take the committees in the order that they are listed in the bylaws. Handle any committee motions as they arise.

Chair: "The next business in order is the report of the Bylaws Committee. Charles Dailey, Chairman."

Bylaws Committee Chairman: "Madam President, proper notice having been given, by direction of the committee, I move the adoption of the following bylaws amendment: Article II, Section 4. subsection a. to strike out the words, 'December 4' and insert the words, 'January 15.'" (A committee motion does not require a second.)

Chair: "The question is on the adoption of the bylaws amendment just presented. That is, to strike out the words, 'December 4' and insert the words, 'January 15' in Article II, Section 4, subsection a. Are you ready for the question?"

(A motion to amend the bylaws is an Incidental Main Motion, and it may be amended just as any main motion, that is, a primary amendment and a secondary amendment may be pending. Then, if the amendments are adopted, the motion to amend the bylaws becomes the amended main motion.)

Chair: "Is there any further amendment or debate?"

Chair: "Amendment of the bylaws requires a two-thirds vote in the affirmative. Those voting in favor of the amendment to the bylaws will rise. Be seated. Those opposed will rise. Be seated. There are two-thirds voting in the affirmative and the amendment is adopted. The committee will report the next amendment."

Bylaws Committee Chairman: "By direction of the committee I move to amend Article V. Section 2. Dues. a. to strike out $45 and insert $75."

Chair: "The question is on the adoption of the bylaws amendment just presented. That is, to amend Article V. Section 2. Dues. a. to strike out $45 and insert $75. Are you ready for the question?" (Motions to amend the amount must be within the scope of the motion, that is, between 45 and 75, not more, not less.)

Member: "Madam President, I move to amend the motion to strike out $75 and insert $70." Another member: "I second the motion."

Chair: "It is moved and seconded to amend the motion by striking out $75 and inserting $70. Is there any discussion?"

Another member: "Madam President, I move to amend the amendment by striking out $70 and inserting $55." (Another member seconds the motion.)

Chair: "It is moved and seconded to amend the amendment by striking out $70 and inserting

$55. Is there any discussion?" (No more amendments are in order at this time. All amendments must be within the scope of the notice. For example, if the dues are now $60, the above amendment would not be in order.)

Chair: "The question is on the adoption of the amendment to the amendment to strike out $70 and inserting $55. Those in favor say aye. Those opposed say no. The ayes have it and the amendment to the amendment is adopted. The question is on the amendment to the main motion to strike out $75 and insert $55. Are you ready for the question?"
Chair: "Those in favor of the amendment to the main motion, say aye. Those opposed, say not. The ayes have it and the amendment is adopted."
Chair: "The question is on the amended main motion to amend the bylaws, Article V. Section 2. Dues.a., by striking out $45 and inserting $55. Adoption of the amendment to the bylaws requires a two-thirds vote in the affirmative. Those voting in favor of the amendment will rise. Be seated. Those voting against the amendment will rise. Be seated. There are two-thirds voting in the affirmative and the bylaws amendment is adopted."

Reports of Special Committees

Chair: "The next business in order is reports of Special Committees. Carolyn Parker will report for the committee appointed by the previous convention to investigate the cost of replacing the computer equipment in the main office and to make recommendations to this convention. Miss Parker."

Committee Chairman: "Madam President, the committee reports that the cost of replacing the computer equipment in the main office with equal quality equipment would be approximately $22,000. However, the equipment has proven to be inadequate to meet the demands of the increased membership, training registration, and publications, and the resulting financial accounting.
The committee recommends, and I move that the Society replace the existing main office computer equipment with a system which has been specially designed for our type of work, and that the Morton Computer Company be retained to replace the equipment at a cost as follows: sale of the existing equipment at $16, 500, and purchase of new equipment at a cost of $47,000."

Chair: "The question is on the adoption of the motion just read. Are there any questions? Is there any further discussion on the motion of the special committee? Those in favor of the motion that the Society replace the existing main office computer equipment with a system which has been specially designed for our type of work, and that the Morton Computer Company be retained to replace the equipment at a cost as follows: sale of the existing equipment at $16, 500, and purchase of new equipment at a cost of $47,000, say aye. Those opposed, say no. The ayes have it and the motion is adopted. The Treasurer is ordered to contact the chairman of the special committee for the details, and to purchase the equipment."

Nominations and Elections

Chair: "The next business in order is an updated Report of the Credentials Committee. Nancy March, Chairman."

Credentials Committee Chairman: "Madam President, the Credentials Committee reports that there are no changes in the credentials report."

Chair: "The next business in order is election of officers for the coming term. The chairman of the Nominating Committee, Jacob Astin, will report."

Nominating Committee Chairman: "The nominating committee places in nomination the following:

For President	Jason Smith
For First Vice President	Ann Bradley
For Second Vice President	Janice Woodson
For Third Vice President	Charles Dailey
For Secretary	Martin Addler
For Treasurer	Charles Sands"

Chair: "You have heard the nominations. They are on page 16 of the printed program. Are there any nominations from the floor for president?"
Are there any nominations from the floor for first vice-president?"
Are there any nominations from the floor for second vice-president?"
Are there any nominations from the floor for third vice-president?"

Member: "Madam President, I nominate Margaret Hansen for third vice-president."

Chair: "Are there any nominations from the floor for secretary?"
Are there any nominations from the floor for treasurer?"

Member: "I nominate Joseph Comstock for Treasurer."

Chair: "Are there any further nominations for any office? There are no further nominations. Nominations are closed. The names of the nominees from the floor are posted on the screen. (Note: have a visible place to post nominees. An overhead projector works well.) Your ballot was issued to you at registration. The Chairman of the Tellers Committee will give instructions on marking and casting your ballot."

Chairman of Tellers: "Beside each name from the nominating committee there is a place to put a check mark. Below that name there is a line to write in another name for that position and a place to put a check mark. Each voting member has one vote for each office. After marking the ballot, please fold it in half, and place it in the ballot box beside the exit door."

Chair: "You have heard the directions for marking, folding, and casting your ballot. Are there any questions? During the voting, the convention will be in recess. The chair declares that according to the bylaws, the polls will be closed in one hour from the time the polls are opened. The chair declares the polls are open and the convention in recess for one hour at which time the polls will be closed and the convention will reconvene."

Reconvene

Chair: "Please be seated. The meeting will come to order. The chairman of the Teller's Committee will report. Betty Charles."

Chairman of Tellers: "The Tellers Committee is not ready at this time to report."

Chair: "Since the Tellers Committee is not ready to report, we will proceed to new business. Is there any new business to come before this convention?"
NOTE: Handle new business the same as you would in a regular meeting. If a motion is made during this time that the bylaws provide for notice, it may be referred to the proper committee, but may not be considered until after notice has been sent.
Chair: "Are the tellers ready to report?"

Chair: "Mrs. Charles will report for the tellers committee."

Chairman of Tellers: "Madam President, the Teller's Committee reports the following:

For President,	Jason Smith received	423
For First Vice President	Ann Bradley received	420
For Second Vice President	Janice Woodson received	382
Write ins:	Margaret Santller received	32
	John Adams received	1
For Third Vice President	Charles Dailey received	230
	Margaret Hansen received	192
For Secretary	Martin Addler received	425
For Treasurer	Charles Sands received	420
	Joseph Comstock received	22.."

NOTE: Chair reads the report, then:

Chair: "The chair declares elected for a term of _____ years:

President	Jason Smith
First Vice President	Ann Bradley
Second Vice President	Janice Woodson
Third Vice President	Charles Dailey
Secretary	Martin Addler
Treasurer	Charles Sands"

Closing exercises

Chair: "The chairman of the Courtesy Resolutions Committee will report."

Note: The committee reads a resolution thanking everyone for their contributions, the convention arrangements committee, the guest speakers, etc. The affirmative vote is taken on adoption of the resolution. No negative vote is taken, unless demanded by a member. This resolution is not necessary. The organization may have other means of thanking everyone for participating.

Chair: "Is there any further business to come before this convention?
There is no further business. The convention is adjourned sine die."

Sample Annual Meeting Agenda

The following agenda is adapted from an actual state association agenda for an annual meeting, with additional notes for you to fill in for you own needs. For this agenda the voting members at the annual meeting are all members with voting rights who attend. For notes, use as much space between items as needed to suit your organization.

Call to order: President_____(time)
Invocation: Chaplain_____
Presentation of Colors: Boy Scout Troop_____

Welcome: Local Chapter President_____
Response: First Vice President_____

Introductions: Those seated at head table: Officers, Secretary, Parliamentarian
          In audience:
          Past State Presidents_____,_____,

          _____,_____

          National President_____

Certification of meeting notice (If required)_____

Report of the Registration Committee_____,Chairman
          Voting members registered _____ Quorum present_____
          Nonvoting association members _____ Guests _____

Report of the Standing Rules Committee_____, Chairman
          (Rules in Program, page 00) *See Appendix IV, page 94.*

Report of the Program Committee_____, Chairman

Minutes approval:
          Appointment of committee to approve minutes of this meeting

          _____,_____,_____

          Report of the committee to approve the minutes of the 1996 annual mtg.

          _____,_____

Appointment of meeting committees
          Tellers_____
          Timekeeper_____
          Doorkeeper_____
          Pages_____
          Resolutions _____
Reports of officers
          President_____
          First Vice President_____

Second Vice President_____

Third Vice President_____

Recording Secretary_____

Corresponding Secretary_____

      Correspondence:

Treasurer_____

Reports of Chapter Presidents _____

Revised report of the Registration Committee_____

Election of officers:

Bylaws election requirements: Secretary read Article X, Officers, Section 2.

Report of Nominating Committee: _____,Chairman

Nominations from the floor: _____

Election:

_____   _____   _____

_____   _____   _____

_____   _____   _____

Report of the Board of Directors: Secretary_____

     "The Board of Directors recommends and I move that a committee be appointed to research the feasibility of selling our current headquarters building and building a new headquarters in the Drew Executive Park."

Questions: call on.   _____, Treasurer, (Carlisle Financial)

                 _____, Board member (Architect)

                 _____, Board member (Douglas Real Estate)

If adopted, appoint committee: First V.P., Ex.Dir., 3 Bd. members

Report of the Executive Director_____

Reports of Standing Committees

    Auditor   _____, Chairman____ADOPT AUDIT

    Budget   _____, Chairman____ADOPT BUDGET

    Bylaws   _____, Chairman____

    Education   _____, Chairman_____

    Membership _____, Chairman: Statistics:_____

Reports of Special Committees

(Tellers Report if ready)

Bylaws amendment: (Proper notice has been given.)

Bylaws Committee Chairman:_____

     "I move to Amend Article VII. Section 3. (2). by striking out "twice every ten years" and inserting "once every three years.""

Report of Seminar Committee:_____,Chairman

Report of Resolutions Committee:_____,Chairman

Unfinished Business and General Orders:
New Business:
Motion: Text

                    Adopted_____Defeated_____
Motion: Text

                    Adopted_____Defeated_____

Presentation of awards: (Optional)
_____:Award_____
_____:Award_____
_____:Award_____

Presentation of certifications of achievement
_____:Certificate_____
_____:Certificate_____
_____:Certificate_____

Thank you to meeting participants, host chapter, _____

Announcements

Adjourn _____(time)

Appendix VI

Chairing a Revision of the Bylaws

A revision of the bylaws is usually undertaken by direction of the assembly. A bylaws revision committee is then appointed to write the document. It is usually better to appoint a separate committee to avoid overburdening the regular bylaws committee.

The bylaws revision committee takes the same care in writing the document as would be taken the first time the organization wrote bylaws. Care should be taken that the language of the document is concise, unambiguous, and says what it means. One or two members should be appointed to edit the new document for errors before it is sent out to members with the notice. *The existing bylaws are in effect until after a revision is adopted.* Amendments to the existing bylaws may be proposed to be considered at the same meeting where the revision will be considered.

At the meeting where the revision will be considered, any amendments proposed to the existing bylaws are considered first.

The chairman of the bylaws revision committee reports: "By direction of the committee I move to substitute the revision for the existing bylaws."

Chair: "The question is on the proposed revision. It will be considered seriatim, section by section. The chairman will read Article I, Section 1."

Chairman reads. Chair: "Is there any debate or amendment on Article I, Section 1?"

During the process of considering the revision, the existing bylaws are not open for debate nor amendment. However, the existing bylaws must be followed for all procedure until the new document is adopted.

The revision is considered seriatim, including the title and Article and Section titles.

The document is open to amendment just as any new main motion. Any paragraph may be amended by first and second degree amendment. New material may be added. The prohibition relating to ordinary bylaws amendments regarding "within the scope of the notice" does not apply to a revision. Anything may be proposed.

If members wish to retain a section of the existing bylaws, *the actual text must be part of the motion to insert, not* such words as "Article III, Section 2 of the existing bylaws."

Require the amendments to be in writing. That is the only way to save time and frustration in amending bylaws. It is the only way to be certain that the words adopted will be the words that appear in the final document. And later, because all amendments were in writing, no member may contend that the printed bylaws were not those which were adopted.

Spend as much time as possible on new amendments from the floor to be certain that the language is careful and in the same style as the bylaws revision. The revision committee chairman may be able to help in wording motions to amend so that they do not conflict with other adopted amendments.

Article and section titles may be amended, as well as their numbers and the outline format.

Amendments from the floor to the proposed revision are adopted by majority vote.

After the entire document has been debated and amended by majority vote, the chair asks: "Are there any further amendments to the proposed revision? Are there any provisos to be presented?"

If any provision in the bylaws is to take effect at a later time, the provisos related to them must be adopted before the revision is adopted. Bylaws take effect immediately upon adoption unless a proviso has been adopted to provide another later time.

"Since there is no further debate or amendment, the question is on the adoption of the revision. Adoption requires a two-thirds vote in the affirmative. Those in favor of adopting the revision will rise. Be seated. (The vote may be counted, and if there are many opposing viewpoints, *the vote should be counted*.) Those voting in the negative will rise. Be seated. There are two-thirds voting in the affirmative and the bylaws revision is adopted." or "There are 276 in the affirmative and 32 in the negative, and the bylaws revision is adopted. The revision just adopted replaces the previous bylaws."

Many organizations retain a professional presiding officer to chair a revision of the bylaws. A revision can be a long and tiring process, and it can be controversial and emotional. A professional presider, as a disinterested party skilled in parliamentary procedure, can help to make it easier for the members to accomplish the task with minimum time and help to avoid unnecessary and repetitive debate.

Script for Revision of Bylaws

Chair: "The next business in order is consideration of the revision of the bylaws. The revision will be considered seriatim, that is, section by section. The chairman of the revision committee will read each section including titles. Members may debate and amend each section and subsection including titles, by majority vote.

When the entire document has been considered this way, members will have another chance to make other amendments. Then a single vote will be taken on adoption of the revision. This will require a two-thirds vote in the affirmative.

The existing bylaws are not germane and will not be considered at all. If any member wishes to retain an item from the existing bylaws, it must be presented in full as a new amendment to the revision. Are there any questions?"

Chair: "Mrs. Dawson, Chairman of the Bylaws Revision Committee, will report."

Mrs. Dawson: "Mister Chairman, by direction of the committee I move to substitute for the existing bylaws the following revision."

Chair: Mrs. "Dawson will read the revision, beginning with Article I, Section 1."

Mrs. Dawson reads.

Chair: "Are there any amendments to Article 1, Section 1? The chair recognizes Mr. Allen."

Mr. Allen: "Mister Chairman, I rise to a point of order."

Chair: "State your point of order."

Mr. Allen: "Mister Chairman, the revision proposes to change the name of the organization. However, we have not been given notice of an amendment to the Articles of Incorporation. The change of name in the bylaws is out of order."

Chair: "Your point is well taken. However, in order to make the correction, the member may propose an amendment."

Mr. Allen: "Mister Chairman, I move to strike out word Medieval and insert the word Renaissance."

Another member seconds the motion.

Chair: "The question is on the motion to amend Article I, Section 1 to strike out the word Medieval and insert the word Renaissance. Are you ready for the question?"

Chair: "Those is favor, say aye. Those opposed, say no. The ayes have it and the amendment is adopted."

Chair: "Is there any further discussion of Article 1, Section 1?"

Chair: "There being no further discussion, Mrs. Dawson will read Article II."

Mrs. Dawson reads.

Chair: "Is there any discussion or amendment of Article II? There being none Mrs. Dawson will read Article III."

Mrs. Dawson reads.

Chair: "Article III is open for amendment. Are you ready for the question?"

Mrs. Calhoun: "Mister Chairman, I move to strike out of Article III, Section 2.D the amount of $5000 and insert $10,000."

Another member seconds the motion.

Chair: "The question is on the motion to amend Article III, Section 2.D. to strike out $5000 and insert $10,000. Are you ready for the question?"

Chair: "The chair recognizes Mr. Jones."

Mr. Jones: "Mister Chairman, it is my belief that if we make the corporate membership contribution too great, we will lose these members and suffer a financial loss. I urge the members to vote against this amendment."

Chair: "Is there any further discussion or amendment?"

Chair: "The question is on the amendment to Article III, Section 2. D. to strike out $5000 and insert $10,000. Those in favor, say aye. Those opposed, say no. The negative has it and the motion to amend is defeated."

Chair: "Is there any further discussion or amendment to Article III? Mrs. Dawson will read Article IV."

(Consideration of the revision continues this way until all articles, sections and subsections have been considered. Then the chair asks if there is any further discussion or amendment to the revision before the final vote is taken.)

Chair: "Is there any further discussion or amendment to any part of the amended revision?"

Chair: "Since there is no further discussion or amendment, the vote on the revision will be taken."

Chair: "The question is on adoption of the revision of the bylaws as amended during this meeting. Are there any provisos to be presented?"

Mrs. Dawson: "Mister Chairman, by direction of the committee, I move that the revision be adopted provided that it shall be in effect at the close of the December meeting."

Chair: "The question is on adoption of the proviso that the revision take effect at the close of the December meeting. Is there any discussion or amendment?"

Chair: "Since there is no discussion or amendment, the question is on adoption of the proviso. Those in favor, say aye. Those opposed, say no. The ayes have it, and the proviso is adopted."

Chair: "The question is on adoption of the revision with the attached proviso. This requires a two-thirds vote in the affirmative. Those in favor will rise, be seated. Those opposed will rise, be seated. There are two-thirds voting in the affirmative and the revision is adopted, and will take effect at the close of the December meeting."

Chair: "The next business in order is announcements. Are there any announcements?"

Mrs. Dawson: "Mister Chairman, the revised bylaws will be published and mailed to members within two weeks."

Chair: "Is there any further business to come before this meeting? There being none, the meeting is adjourned."

If this is a special meeting to consider the revision, no other business may be conducted. Then the chair would adjourn the meeting without the phrase "Is there any further business to come before this meeting?"

This is the general tone of consideration of a revision. As is demonstrated, the revision may take several hours to complete. Sufficient time should be allowed for the revision, so that it will not be necessary to hold an adjourned meeting to finish it.

Appendix VII

Bylaw Amendments
Short Perspective

Basic Bylaws Articles
Article I - Name
Article II - Object
Article III - Members
Article IV - Officers
Article V - Meetings
Article VI - Executive Board (Board of Directors)
Article VII - Committees
Article VIII - Parliamentary Authority
Article IX - Amendment of Bylaws

Amendment of Bylaws

Amendment of bylaws requires notice and a two-thirds vote for adoption unless the bylaws require otherwise. *Notice* must be given according to the provisions of the bylaws or statutes.

When the amendments are considered by the assembly, only the proposed amendments are before the assembly for consideration. The remainder of the bylaws may not be amended at that time, because notice was not given.

To amend the bylaws is an *Incidental Main Motion*, which means that the motion is debatable and amendable. Amendments from the floor to the proposal must be germane and within the *scope of the notice*. For example, the bylaws might state that the board of directors shall consist of twenty-five directors. The proposed amendment is to change that number to twelve. Amendments from the floor must be within the scope of the notice, that is, between twenty-five and twelve. A change of more than twenty-five or less than twelve is not in order.

If the bylaws amendment proposes to change a provision that is listed in more than one place in the bylaws, the proposal in the notice should include all places where change is desired, including the renumbering of articles, sections and subsections.

Procedure: The Chair introduces the next business in order:
"The next business in order is the proposed amendment of the bylaws. Mark Redact will report for the Bylaws Committee."

The committee chairman reads the proposed amendments and moves their adoption. Chair: "The question is on the adoption of the amendments to the bylaws. The amendments will be considered seriatim, that is, one section at a time." "The first amendment is … . Are you ready for the question?"

Amendments from the floor to the proposed amendment are adopted by a majority vote. All amendments to the proposed amendment must be germane and within the scope of the notice. After all proposed amendments have been debated and amended, the amended amendment is adopted by a two-thirds vote. Unrelated amendments may be adopted separately.

The adopted amendment of the bylaws goes into effect immediately unless a proviso (to have another time for the bylaws amendment to go into effect) is adopted by a majority vote before the amendment itself is adopted by the required two-thirds vote.

An affirmative vote on adoption of bylaws amendments may not be reconsidered, although a negative vote may.

Luck is where opportunity meets preparation.

For a thorough explanation of the process of writing and amending bylaws see *Bylaws: Writing, Adopting, Amending* by the same author and available from Frederick Publishers.

Bylaws Amendments - General Orders
Script

Chair: "The next business in order is the consideration of the proposed bylaw amendment. Mr. Carrie, Chairman of the Bylaws Committee, will report."

Mr. Carrie: "Madam President, by direction of the committee I move the adoption of the following amendment to the bylaws:
Article III. Section 2.a. _____"

Chair: "The question is on the proposed amendment to Article III. Section 2.a. Are you ready for the question?"

(Members may now ask questions, debate, and propose amendments from the floor to the proposed amendment.)

Member: "Madam President, I move to amend the proposed amendment by striking out ___ and inserting_____."

Second.

Chair: "The question is on the motion to amend the proposed amendment by striking out _____ and inserting _____. Are you ready for the question?" or
"Is there any discussion or amendment?"

Chair: "Those in favor of adopting the amendment to the proposed bylaw amendment, say aye. Those opposed, say no. The ayes have it and the amendment is adopted. The amended bylaws amendment now reads '_____'"

Chair: "The question is on the adoption of the amended amendment to the bylaws. Are you ready for the question?"

(Further amendment is in order as long as the amendments are germane and within the scope of the notice.)

Chair: "Is there any further debate or amendment?"

Chair: "The question is on the adoption of the bylaw amendment as amended. Those in favor of adopting the bylaw amendment will rise. Be seated. Those opposed will rise. Be seated. There are two-thirds voting in the affirmative and the bylaw amendment as amended is adopted."

Chair: "Is there any new business to come before this meeting?"

(Continue with the usual order of business.)

Bibliography

Delinger, Susan, and Barbara Deane. *Communicating Effectively*. Radnor, PA: Chilton, 1980.

Demeter, George. *Demeter's Manual of Parliamentary Law and Procedure*. Boston: Little, Brown, 1969.

Dunbar, Peter M. *The Condominium Concept.* Tallahassee, FL: Suncoast Professional Publishing Corp., 1996.

Everitt, Lala. *The Facts. A Guide for Writing and Amending Bylaws*. Dallas: Lee Books.

Fiedler, Fred E., et al. *Improving Leadership Effectiveness*. New York: John Wiley & Sons, 1976.

Hayakawa, S. I. *Language in Thought and Action*, 4th Ed. New York: Harcourt, 1978.

Robert, Sarah Corbin, et al. *Robert's Rules of Order Newly Revised*. Glenview, IL: Scott Foresman, 1990.

Stephens, Joyce L. *Basic Parliamentary Procedure Workbook*. 5th Ed. Clearwater, FL: Frederick Publishers, 1994.

Stephens, Joyce L. *Guide to Voting Procedures*. Clearwater, FL: Frederick Publishers, 1993.

Stephens, Joyce L. *Bylaws: Writing, Amending, Revising*. Clearwater, FL: Frederick Publishers, 1996.

Stephens, Joyce L. *Guide to Elections*. Clearwater, FL: Frederick Publishers, 1997.

Weinland, James D. *How to Think Straight*. Totowa, NJ: Littlefield, Adams: 1980.

Index

- **Other books by Joyce L. Stephens**
- **Available from Frederick Publishers**

BASIC PARLIAMENTARY PROCEDURE WORKBOOK, 5th Edition

Written by a Professional Registered Parliamentarian, this book is essentially a basic course in parliamentary procedure, written for beginners and others who want to sharpen their skills. Much more than a list of the rules, this book explains key words and phrases, and provides common examples, samples of rules, reports, minutes, actual language to use, and quizzes to test your knowledge.
The easy-to-read format will guide you painlessly through:
• How to make a motion • How to write a resolution • Nominations and elections • Duties of officers and committees • How to write minutes • Voting, quorum, seconding and more.
Paper 8.5 x 11   ISBN 0-9629765-4-7 $15.95

GUIDE TO VOTING
Procedures for Voluntary Organizations

A single source for information about and procedures for all methods of voting: voice, ballot, proxy, preferential, cumulative, teleconference, machine, bullet voting, secret ballot by mail and more. Included is a chapter on voting in governmental elections, direct voting and electoral college. This book is a valuable resource for individuals and organizations for all voting procedures.
Paper 8.5 x 11   ISBN 0-9629765-3-9 $24.95

BYLAWS: WRITING, AMENDING, REVISING

How to write understandable and usable bylaws using a simple and tested formula; How to write and adopt amendments without causing more problems; how to chair a meeting to consider amendments or a revision; how to instruct committees; how to write and adopt a revision; and scripts for handling these and other motions.
Spiral bound 8.5 x 11   ISBN 0-9629765-8-X $14.95

Guide to Elections: Procedures for Voluntary Organizations
available 10/97   Spiral bound 8.5 x 11   ISBN 0-9629765-9-8 $14.95

Order Form
Books by Joyce L. Stephens

Basic Parliamentary Procedure Workbook ____ @ $15.95 ea._____

Guide For The Presiding Officer, 2nd ed. ____ @ $19.95 ea._____

Guide to Voting Procedures (Nonprofit Organizations) ____ @ $24.95 ea._____

Bylaws: Writing, Adopting, Amending (Spiral) ____ @ $14.95 ea._____

Guide to Elections (Nonprofit Orgs.)(Spiral)(Oct 1997) ____ @ $14.95 ea._____

Florida residents please add appropriate sales tax _____

10% discount for two or more books mailed to the same address _____

Total Enclosed _____

Postage, shipping, handling
One book $3.00
   Additional books add $.50 each Postage and handling _____

Total enclosed _____

Name _____

Address _____

State_____Zip Code_____Phone _____

Organization _____

Make check payable to: Frederick Publishers
Mail to Frederick Publishers at:
P. O. Box 5043
Clearwater, FL 33758
Information (813) 530-3978